Holistic Education Redefined: The Educational Philosophy of Prof. Achyuta Samanta

(3 R's, 3 H's & 3 E's)

Holistic Education Redefined: The Educational Philosophy of Prof. Achyuta Samanta

(3 R's, 3 H's & 3 E's)

Dr. Rasmi Ranjan Puhan
Assistant Professor of Education,
Government Teachers' Training College,
Phulbani, Kandhamal, Odisha

Dr. Lakshmipriya Malla
Assistant Professor of Education,
Head of the Department (HOD),
Government Autonomous College,
Phulbani, Kandhamal, Odisha

BLACK EAGLE BOOKS
Dublin, USA | Bhubaneswar, India

 Black Eagle Books
USA address:
7464 Wisdom Lane
Dublin, OH 43016

India address:
E/312, Trident Galaxy, Kalinga Nagar,
Bhubaneswar-751003, Odisha, India

E-mail: info@blackeaglebooks.org
Website: www.blackeaglebooks.org

First International Edition Published by
Black Eagle Books, 2025

**Holistic Education Redefined: The Educational Philosophy
of Prof. Achyuta Samanta (3 R's, 3 H's & 3 E's)
by Dr. Rasmi Ranjan Puhan | Dr. Lakshmipriya Malla**

Copyright © Authors

All rights reserved. No part of this publication may be reproduced, stored in a retrieval system, or transmitted, in any form or by any means, electronic, mechanical, photocopying, recording or otherwise without the prior permission of the publisher.

Cover & Interior Design: Ezy's Publication

ISBN- 978-1-64560-691-8 (Paperback)

Printed in the United States of America

DEDICATION

We humbly dedicate this book, *Holistic Education Redefined* (**3 H's, 3 R's & 3 E's**) *: Educational Philosophy of Prof. Achyuta Samanta*, to **Lord Jagannath**, the eternal source of wisdom and divine guidance.

With profound love and gratitude, we also dedicate this work to **all my lovable KISSians**, whose unwavering spirit, resilience, and pursuit of knowledge continue to inspire me every day. You are the true embodiment of education's transformative power.

May this book serve as a small tribute to the boundless grace of the Lord and the indomitable will of the KISS family.

Dr. Rasmi Ranjan Puhan & Dr. Lakshmipriya Malla

Preface

Education is the cornerstone of human development, and its transformative power is most evident when it reaches the underprivileged. **Prof. Achyuta Samanta**, a visionary social activist and philanthropist, has redefined the landscape of education for marginalized communities through his pioneering institution, the **Kalinga Institute of Social Sciences (KISS)**. His life and work exemplify a profound commitment to **holistic education**, ensuring that poor tribal students receive not only academic knowledge but also the values, skills, and opportunities needed to thrive in an ever-changing world.

We are truly overwhelmed and astonished by the extraordinary **KISS Model**, which has transformed **indigenous students** into **leaders across various fields**. **Holistic Education**, which was once a mere dream for many educationists and nations, is being realized in its truest form through this remarkable initiative.

This book is a humble attempt to document the life philosophy and educational vision of **Prof. Samanta**—a man who turned his personal struggles into an unwavering mission for social upliftment. His unique approach to education integrates knowledge, values, skill development, and well-being, ensuring that the students of KISS are not only educated but also empowered to lead dignified and self-reliant lives. The journey of KISS is a testament to the power of compassion and perseverance. It showcases how one individual's commitment can create a sustainable model for inclusive and Holistic Education, creating pathways for economic and social empowerment, and ensuring opportunities for generations to come. **Prof. Samanta's holistic approach serves as an inspiration to educators, policymakers, and change-**

makers worldwide. **Prof. Samanta's story is not just an inspiration but a blueprint for change**, demonstrating how education can be a powerful tool for breaking the cycle of poverty and empowering generations. His philosophy integrates academic excellence with **moral and social responsibility**, proving that true education goes beyond textbooks and classrooms to nurture the intellect, character, and emotional well-being of learners.

This book, **Holistic Education Redefined (3H's, 3R's & 3E's): Educational Philosophy of Prof. Achyuta Samanta**, is a humble attempt to analyze and celebrate this unique educational model that **aligns seamlessly with the vision of NEP-2020 and UN Sustainable Goal**. With India now prioritizing **holistic, inclusive, and skill-based education**, this work will serve as a valuable academic resource for students pursuing **M.A., M.Phil., Ph.D. in Education, as well as Social Science and Humanities**, as well as those in **teacher education programs like B.Ed. and M.Ed., making it a reliable source for interdisciplinary studies**.

We extend our sincere gratitude to all who have contributed to this book and to those who continue to support the noble cause of Holistic and **inclusive education**. May this work serve as both a tribute to **Prof. Samanta's vision** and a call to action for educators, policymakers, and change-makers worldwide?

Dr. Rasmi Ranjan Puhan &
Dr. Lakshmipriya Malla

Table of Contents

Chapter	Particulars	Page No.
1	KISS Through the Lens of Leaders and Luminaries from Around the Globe	13
	Nobel Laureates	
	Legal Luminaries	
	International Dignitaries	
	Policymakers	
	Spiritual Leaders	
	Celebrities	
	Closing Note	
2	KISS at a Glance	35
	Introduction	
3	Brief Sketch of Life History	39
	His Struggling Life to Becoming a Legend (as an Educational Entrepreneur)	
4	His Vision	44
5	His Great Achievements	45
	• National Recognition as a Member	
	• National Recognition as a Serving Member	
	• International Recognition as a Serving Member	
	• Recognition and Appreciation (Academics)	
	• Honoris Causa: D. Litt & D.Sc	
	• Mention in Record Books	
	• Recognition and Appreciation (Social Sector)	
6	His Philosophy of Life	58
	• Art of Giving	
7	Impact of His Philosophy and Social Work on Society	60
	• Birth of the Incredible Educational Institution KISS	
	• Real Transformation of Tribals	
	• Changing Impressions of the Highest Possibilities	
	• Qualitative Change in Tribal Uplift	
	• International Journey and Achievements of Tribals	
	• KISS Touches the Hearts of World Leaders and Renowned Activists	
	• Recognizing Service to Humanity Globally	
	• Service to Mother and Motherland	

Chapter	Particulars	Page No.
	• Strengthening Art and Culture	
	• Strengthening Local Economy	
	• Preaching Simple Living and High Thinking	
	• Promoting "Service to Mankind is Service to God"	
8	His Philosophy of Education (Holistic Education)	71
	Key pillars of his educational philosophy include	
	• Meaning of Education	
	• Definition of Education	
9	The Mission of Life Through Education	80
	• Key Components of His Mission Through Education	
	• **Alignment with Millennium Development Goals (MDGs)**	
	• **Alignment with Sustainable Development Goals (SDGs)**	
10	Holistic Education Centre – KISS	112
	• Introduction	
	• Dream of Education as KISS	
	Overview of KISS Campus	
	Satellite Centres: Expanding Horizons for Education and Service to Mankind	
	KISS: A Global Beacon of Hope and Equality for Tribal Children journey so far…	
	Concept of Holistic Education	
	• Meaning of Holistic Education	
	Prof. Samants's Holistic Education: Blending the 3 H's, 3 R's, and 3 E's	
	Philosophical Foundations of Holism in Education: Achyuta Samanta's Perspective *(Metaphysics, Epistemology, and Axiology)*	
	Achyuta Samanta as the Father of Holism in 21st-Century Education	
	Holistic Human Development Model	
11	Aims of Education	114
	• Service to Mankind	
	• Simple Living and High Thinking	
	• Stress on Practical Life Skills/Practical Education for Self-Reliance	
	• Universal Education	
	• All-Round Development of Personality	

Chapter	Particulars	Page No.
	• Spiritual Development	
	• Development of Inventive and Creative Power	
	• Aesthetic Development	
	• Vocational Self-Reliance: Building a Sustainable Future	
	• Education for Employability and Life Skills	
	• Preservation and Transmission of Culture	
	• Empowerment of Women	
12	Curriculum	157
	• Common Syllabus for All-Round Development	
	• Vocational Education	
	• Training in Games and Sports	
	• Art and Craft Education	
	• Multilingual Education	
	• Language Education (with Language Lab)	
	• Life-Skill Education	
	• Employment-Based Education	
	• Micro-English Access Program	
	• Cultural Education	
13	Methods of Teaching	179
	• Play-Way Method	
	• Heuristic Method	
	• Experiential and Active Learning	
	• Problem-Solving	
	• Project Method	
	• Maxims of Teaching	
14	Role of Teacher	200
	• Role as Teacher	
	• Role as Mentor	
	• Role as Tutor	
	• Role in Dining-Based Duty and Roster	
	• Role as Supervisor	
	• Role as Organizer	
	• Role as Controller	
	• Role as Planner	
	• Role as Manager	

Chapter	Particulars	Page No.
15	Holistic Education and Students	215
16	Holistic Education and School	216
17	Discipline	218
18	Contribution of Prof. Achyuta Samanta to the Indian Education System	221
19	Conclusion	223
20	Comprehensive and Differential Comparison between Holistic and Integral Education	224
	Bibliography	226

✱✱✱

KISS Through the Lens of Leaders and Luminaries from Around the Globe

Nobel Laureates

The Kalinga Institute of Social Sciences (KISS), founded by the visionary Prof. Achyuta Samanta, stands as a testament to the power of education in transforming lives and building an equitable society. Recognized as a global model for holistic education and social inclusion, KISS has garnered accolades from Nobel Laureates who have visited the institution. Their words of admiration reflect the universal significance of KISS's mission and its profound impact on addressing poverty, inequality, and education for the underprivileged.

Prof. Rolf M. Zinkernagel
Nobel Laureate in Medicine (1996)
Prof. Rolf M. Zinkernagel, during his visit to KISS, expressed his deep appreciation for the institution's efforts in empowering underprivileged children through education. He remarked:
"KISS is an extraordinary initiative to try to educate children. I think particularly girls, it is very important to educate them."
His statement underscores the vital role KISS plays in promoting gender equality and ensuring access to education for all, reflecting the institution's commitment to creating a better and more inclusive future.

Prof. Richard R. Ernst
Nobel Laureate in Chemistry (1991)
Prof. Richard R. Ernst, while reflecting on the transformative work of KISS and the visionary leadership of Prof. Achyuta Samanta, shared his profound respect and admiration. He remarked:
"Dr. Samanta is a life model for me."
This succinct yet powerful statement captures the inspiration drawn from Prof. Samanta's dedication to holistic education at KISS, which has become a global model for empowering marginalized communities and transforming lives.

Prof. Ferid Murad
Nobel Laureate in Physiology or Medicine (1998)
Prof. Ferid Murad, upon witnessing the transformative work of KISS and Prof. Achyuta Samanta's visionary leadership, expressed deep admiration for the institution's impact. He eloquently stated:
"What is Education? Education is very precious. What Dr. Samanta has done is more than a couple of pounds of gold."
His words highlight not only the immense value of education but also the unparalleled contribution Dr. Samanta has made in creating a holistic educational framework that serves the most underserved communities, far beyond material wealth.

Prof. Ada Etil Yonath
Nobel Laureate in Chemistry, 2009 (Israel)
Prof. Ada Etil Yonath, during her visit to KISS, was deeply impressed by the scale and impact of the institution. Reflecting on the parallels with her home country, she remarked:
"My country, Israel, has 25,000 students, but here at KISS, I see the same numbers. KISS is really impressive."
Her statement highlights the magnitude of KISS's reach and its unparalleled commitment to providing education to thousands of underprivileged children. It underscores the institution's global significance as a model of holistic education and empowerment.

Prof. Muhammad Yunus
Nobel Peace Prize Winner, 2006
Prof. Muhammad Yunus, renowned for his pioneering work in social entrepreneurship and microfinance, expressed profound admiration for KISS during his visit. He remarked:
"KISS is a wonder. It is rare in the world."
These powerful words from the Nobel Peace Prize laureate encapsulate the uniqueness of KISS as a global model of holistic education, breaking barriers and transforming the lives of countless underprivileged children. His statement underscores the institution's unparalleled contribution to creating a more inclusive and equitable society.

Prof. Hiroshi Amano
Nobel Laureate in Physics, 2014

Prof. Hiroshi Amano, while reflecting on the extraordinary accomplishments of KISS and the vision of Prof. Achyuta Samanta, expressed his heartfelt admiration. He remarked:

"Your achievement is just incredible and extremely difficult to emulate for generations to come."

This profound statement from the esteemed Nobel Laureate underscores the unparalleled legacy of KISS as a global model of holistic education and social transformation, setting a benchmark that inspires future generations worldwide.

Prof. Erwin Neher
Nobel Laureate in Physiology or Medicine, 1991

Prof. Erwin Neher, deeply moved by the vision and efforts of KISS, praised the institution's transformative role in shaping the future. He remarked:

"It's really amazing that KISS is working for the benefit of future generations. It is putting thousands of students on the right track."

His words reflect the profound impact of KISS in empowering underprivileged children through education and creating a brighter, more equitable future for generations to come.

Prof. Olivier Smithies
Nobel Laureate in Physiology or Medicine, 2007

Prof. Olivier Smithies, during his visit to KISS, shared a heartfelt reflection on the scale and impact of the institution. Drawing a comparison to his own humble beginnings, he remarked:

"You know, I come from a small village. You are 10 times the size of my village."

His words highlight the incredible magnitude of KISS and its ability to bring together thousands of children under one roof, transforming their lives through holistic education and opportunities. It serves as a powerful testament to the institution's far-reaching impact and vision.

Sir Richard John Roberts
Nobel Laureate in Physiology or Medicine, 1993

Sir Richard John Roberts, deeply moved by the extraordinary achievements of KISS, expressed his heartfelt admiration for the visionary leadership of Prof. Achyuta Samanta. He remarked:

"I am overwhelmed with admiration to witness what Prof. Achyuta Samanta has created through his vision, dedication, and passion."

These powerful words capture the profound respect and inspiration evoked by Prof. Samanta's relentless efforts to transform lives through education. KISS stands as a living testament to his unwavering commitment to empowering the underprivileged and creating a brighter future.

Shri Kailash Satyarthi
Nobel Peace Prize Winner, 2014

Shri Kailash Satyarthi, a global champion of children's rights, was deeply moved by his visit to KISS. Reflecting on the joy and hope radiating from the students, he shared:

"It's a pleasure to see the smiling faces of the children here at KISS. Visiting KISS is like a pilgrimage. Temple, Mosque, and Church all reside in the smiles of these innocent children."

His profound words celebrate the unity in diversity that KISS embodies, blending the spirit of India's cultural heritage with a mission to uplift and empower underprivileged children. For millions, KISS is not just an institution—it is a sacred space where education transforms lives and nurtures the soul of the nation

Prof. Ernesto Kahan
Nobel Peace Prize Winner, 1985

Prof. Ernesto Kahan, during his visit to KISS and KIIT, expressed his deep admiration for the institution's vision and infrastructure. He remarked:

"I am very impressed with the facilities at KISS and KIIT. I wish KISS to grow and be able to be a good example to the world."

His statement reflects the global significance of KISS

as a pioneering institution that sets a benchmark for holistic education and empowerment. Prof. Kahan's words inspire KISS to continue its remarkable journey of transforming lives and serving as a beacon of hope for the underprivileged worldwide.

Prof. Jean-Marie Lehn
Nobel Laureate in Chemistry, 1987
Prof. Jean-Marie Lehn, during his visit to KISS, highlighted the universal significance of education as the foundation for progress and transformation. Deeply impressed by the institution's mission, he remarked:
"Education of these young children is fantastic because everything starts with education. We would not exist here in this room without education. I think this is the most important thing."
His profound words underscore the global relevance of KISS as a model institution, demonstrating how access to quality education can empower marginalized communities and shape a brighter, more inclusive future for humanity.

Legal Luminaries

Dr. Justice Dalveer Bhandari,
Judge at the International Court of Justice
During his visit, he eloquently captures the essence of Kalinga Institute of Social Sciences (KISS) as a beacon of holistic education and social transformation. Having traversed over 50 countries globally, Dr. Bhandari acknowledges the unparalleled uniqueness of KISS, a sanctuary of inclusive education empowering underprivileged tribal students. He remarks,
"KISS is unique. I have been to more than 50 countries in the world and I have spent time in some of the countries much longer, but I have not come across such institution anywhere in the world. We salute Dr. Samanta for seeing a dream and translating it into reality with determination."
KISS stands as a testament to the power of education in fostering equality, dignity, and sustainable development, earning admiration from global dignitaries like Dr. Bhandari.

Justice Antonio Augusto Cancado Trindade
Judge at the International Court of Justice

visited Kalinga Institute of Social Sciences (KISS) and was deeply moved by its groundbreaking work in providing education to marginalized tribal communities. Addressing the students, Justice Trindade shared his profound insights, remarking,
"Dear students, you have a unique opportunity in education, which is vital not only for your personal growth but also for understanding the world around you—the world in which we live."
These words reflect his deep appreciation of the holistic approach at KISS, which integrates academic excellence with cultural, ethical, and social values, fostering a comprehensive understanding of the interconnected world

His Excellency Dr. Abdulqawi Ahmed Yusuf,
Vice President of the International Court of Justice

He expressed his profound admiration for Kalinga Institute of Social Sciences (KISS), recognizing it as a trailblazing institution in the realm of social transformation. Speaking about its extraordinary mission, he remarked,
"KISS, in my view, constitutes a unique experiment in social transformation. It has a remarkably distinctive mission of lifting tens of thousands of children out of poverty and illiteracy and giving them the gift of education and life-long skills. Dr. Samanta has inspired me to start a KISS in Somalia."
These words from a global luminary not only highlight the unparalleled work of KISS but also underscore the visionary leadership of Prof. Achyuta Samanta in creating a model of holistic education that transcends borders. Dr. Yusuf's intention to replicate KISS in Somalia speaks volumes about the institution's impact, serving as a beacon of hope and a catalyst for change in creating a better, more equitable world.

International Dignitaries

Mr. Gianni Infantino,
President of FIFA,

He recognized the remarkable efforts of KIIT and KISS in advancing sports education and infrastructure, He remarked,

"I am informed that KIIT & KISS have been creating sports infrastructure, hand-holding sportspersons, and promoting sports comprehensively since 2005 under the able guidance of visionary Dr. Achyuta Samanta. I am also told that three students of KIIT participated in the 2020 Tokyo Olympics and believe KIIT and KISS will send a bigger contingent in years to come."

Mr. Infantino's words serve as a testament to the integral role that sports play in the holistic education framework at KISS. Beyond academics, KISS emphasizes physical fitness, teamwork, and character-building through its comprehensive sports programs, empowering students to excel both on the field and in life. The institution's consistent investment in sports infrastructure and its support for athletes underscores the holistic approach at KISS, where academic growth, physical development, and personal empowerment go hand in hand, ensuring that students are well-rounded and ready to tackle global challenges.

Mr. Virendra Sharma
Hon'ble Member of Parliament from the UK (2023)

He, expressed deep admiration and respect for the visionary work of Dr. Achyuta Samanta, emphasizing the profound impact of his contributions. He passionately stated,

"I want to congratulate Dr. Achyuta Samanta for his exceptional work in bringing his vision to life through the institutions he has founded. The achievements he has made are nothing short of awe-inspiring, and we should all learn from him."

Mr. Sharma's words resonate with immense reverence for Dr. Samanta's tireless dedication and transformative leadership, particularly in the realm of holistic education. The institutions founded by Dr. Samanta go beyond traditional academic learning; they focus on nurturing the mind, body, and spirit, setting new benchmarks in education, empowerment, and social development. Dr. Samanta's vision encompasses not just intellectual growth but also character-building, physical well-being, and emotional resilience, ensuring that every student is prepared to thrive in all aspects of life.

Mr. Robert Pittenger,
Former US Congressman from North Carolina

He profoundly acknowledged the transformative impact of Dr. Achyuta Samanta, likening his work to that of a modern-day Mother Teresa. He remarked,

"If we had more Dr. Samanta's in the world today, it would be a different world. He is a modern day Mother Teresa. If he were a Catholic, we would have made him a saint."

These words speak volumes about Dr. Samanta's unwavering dedication to holistic education and his relentless pursuit of social transformation. His commitment to uplifting the marginalized through education and empowering communities with knowledge, compassion, and life skills embodies the essence of holistic education. Dr. Samanta's visionary approach not only redefines education but also exemplifies how one individual's efforts can reshape the world, making it more inclusive, compassionate, and just for all.

UK Baroness Prashar,
Member of the House of Lords

During her visit she expressed deep admiration for the transformative impact of Kalinga Institute of Social Sciences (KISS), recognizing it as a beacon of inspiration in her career. She remarked,

"This institution has inspired me the most in the whole of my working career. Prof. Samanta's vision has made it a reality, and by emphasizing women empowerment, he is following Mahatma Gandhi's ideals."

Baroness Prashar's words highlight the core principles of holistic education at KISS, where the emphasis is not only on academic excellence but also on social responsibility, gender equality, and empowerment. Dr. Achyuta Samanta's vision of uplifting marginalized communities and empowering women aligns with the ideals of Mahatma Gandhi, promoting values of equality, compassion, and self-reliance. KISS embodies a holistic approach, nurturing students in mind, body, and spirit, while fostering a sense of purpose to contribute meaningfully to society. Dr. Samanta's leadership has not only created an institution of academic distinction but also one that serves as a powerful force for positive social change.

Rt. Hon. Sir Anerood Jugnauth
His Excellency, the President of Mauritius,
Expressed his profound admiration for the transformative work of Dr. Achyuta Samanta and the institutions of KISS and KIIT. He stated,

"After having taken cognizance of the amount and effort being put in by Dr. Samanta and the staff of KISS and KIIT, I am very impressed. I had never thought that social service on such a large scale could be organized to come to the assistance of children of the less privileged members of society."

President Jugnauth's words reflect his awe at the scale and impact of the social service initiatives led by Dr. Samanta. KISS, through its commitment to holistic education, Dr. Samanta's visionary leadership has created an environment where education is not just a tool for knowledge acquisition, but a means of transforming lives, lifting children from underprivileged backgrounds, and empowering them to become agents of change in society. Through this unique model of holistic education, KISS stands as a shining example of how large-scale social service, driven by education, can uplift entire communities and foster a more inclusive, compassionate world.

His Excellency Lyonchhen Jigmi Y. Thinley
Hon'ble Prime Minister,
The Royal Government of Bhutan

During his vist to KISS he recognized the profound humanitarian impact of Dr. Achyuta Samanta, stating, *"Dr. Samanta is one of the greatest humanitarians in the world today. KISS is realizing humanitarian dream of quality education for marginalized children."Your education here – your admission, your food, your hostel"*

These powerful words reflect the global admiration for Dr. Samanta's relentless dedication to transforming the lives of marginalized communities through education. His visionary leadership has transcended borders, creating a ripple effect of positive change that uplifts the underprivileged and empowers them to break free from cycles of poverty and illiteracy.

Mr. Timothy J. Roemer
His Excellency the US Ambassador To India

His Excellency expressed deep admiration for the leadership and vision at KIIT and KISS, remarking,
"I am so deeply inspired by the leadership at KIIT and KISS and the selfless example of providing opportunity for students to live out their dreams."

His words reflect the essence of holistic education at KISS, where every student is given the tools to grow not only intellectually but also socially, emotionally, and ethically. Through a comprehensive approach that nurtures all aspects of a student's development, KISS empowers underprivileged communities to realize their potential and pursue their dreams. The selfless leadership of Dr. Achyuta Samanta ensures that education becomes a transformative force, uplifting individuals and fostering a brighter, more inclusive future for all. Mr. Roemer's admiration underscores the global recognition of KISS as a model for holistic education that truly changes lives.

His Excellency Mr. Rajkeswur Purryag, GCSK, GOSK
President of the Republic of Mauritius

His Excellency, eloquently recognized the far-reaching impact of Dr. Achyuta Samanta's work, stating,
"Education, inequity, marginalization, poverty, sustainability, empowerment, peace, and environment are central to Dr. Samanta's work that it is a highly commendable achievement in today's world."

These words encapsulate the core values of holistic education at KISS, where Dr. Samanta's vision goes beyond conventional learning. His work addresses the multifaceted challenges facing marginalized communities, integrating education with social equity, empowerment, and sustainability. Dr. Samanta's efforts to create a model of education that fosters peace, environmental stewardship, and social justice underscore the transformative power of holistic education in shaping a more inclusive and harmonious world.

Mr. Yuri Afanasiev
UN Resident Coordinator and UNDP Resident Representative, India
He expressed his awe at the incredible achievement of Kalinga Institute of Social Sciences (KISS), stating,
"It is difficult to imagine how such a colossal organization has been set up without government support. It will go a long way in furthering the rights of tribal children globally."
His words underscore the remarkable impact of KISS in empowering marginalized tribal communities through holistic education. Despite limited external support, Dr. Achyuta Samanta's unwavering vision and commitment have created an institution that stands as a beacon for the rights of tribal children, providing them with opportunities for education, empowerment, and social mobility. KISS not only transforms individual lives but also sets a precedent for addressing global inequalities, proving that education can be a powerful tool for advancing the rights and well-being of underprivileged communities worldwide.

Policymakers

Dr. A.P.J. Abdul Kalam
Former President of India

He extended his heartfelt congratulations to Dr. Achyuta Samanta for founding transformative institutions like KIIT and KISS, which embody excellence and values. He remarked,
"I congratulate Dr. Samanta for establishing institutions of character like KIIT and KISS. I urge the students of KIIT & KISS to take the lead in spreading the message of peace and non-violence in today's strife-torn world."
These words reflect Dr. Kalam's deep admiration for the visionary leadership of Dr. Samanta and the holistic education imparted at KISS. By nurturing students with not just academic knowledge but also moral values, these institutions empower them to become ambassadors of peace, compassion,

and non-violence in a world grappling with conflict and divisions. where education serves as a force for unity, harmony, and global progress, inspiring students to contribute meaningfully to building a better, more peaceful world.

Smt. Pratibha Devisingh Patil,
Hon'ble Former President of India,
She expressed her deep admiration for Dr. Achyuta Samanta, describing him
"a great saint and a great gift to society."
These simple yet profound words encapsulate the essence of Dr. Samanta's life and mission. Through his visionary leadership, he has transformed Kalinga Institute of Social Sciences (KISS) into a global model of holistic education, empowering marginalized communities with dignity and opportunity. Her words serve as a tribute to the transformative power of education and the indelible legacy of a leader devoted to building a more compassionate and equitable world.

Shri Narendra Modi
Prime Minister of India

Hon'ble Prime Minister of India, extended his heartfelt appreciation for the visionary efforts of Dr. Achyuta Samanta, stating,
"I wholeheartedly appreciate Dr. Achyuta Samanta and the cause of promoting education for the tribal population and ushering in a positive change for them."
"The way KISS is trying to change the lives of tribal people in a positive way by providing education is very important. Babasaheb Dr. Bhimrao Ambedkar had always given importance on the kind of upliftment through education of tribal, Dalits and other backward classes."
These words highlight the profound impact of Dr. Samanta's mission to uplift marginalized tribal communities through the transformative power of education. Kalinga Institute of Social Sciences (KISS) stands as a shining example of his dedication, providing a holistic educational model that nurtures intellectual growth, cultural preservation, and social empowerment. Prime Minister Modi's recognition underscores the importance of this unparalleled initiative, which continues to inspire and bring lasting change to countless lives across the nation.

Shri M. Hamid Ansari
Vice President of India

He expressed his profound admiration for the remarkable achievements of Kalinga Institute of Social Sciences (KISS), stating,
"KISS far exceeds what I had heard about it. Dr. Samanta has demonstrated that if one has passion to do something for the society, a lot can be done."

These powerful words reflect the unparalleled impact of Dr. Achyuta Samanta's visionary leadership and unwavering commitment to social transformation. KISS is a testament to how passion, dedication, and a clear vision can create an institution that not only provides holistic education to marginalized communities but also empowers them to break the cycle of poverty and achieve self-reliance.

Shri Ram Jethmalani
Hon'ble Member of Parliament (R.S.) and Senior Advocate, Supreme Court of India

His profound admiration for Kalinga Institute of Social Sciences (KISS) and its visionary founder, Dr. Achyuta Samanta. He remarked with deep reverence,
"KISS is a great institution. I express my great sense of satisfaction and pride that I have been introduced to the Founder. I have already become his disciple. He looks such a simple creature but is a divine creation, and, I think, he is a bit of God himself."
These heartfelt words highlight the extraordinary impact of Dr. Samanta's selfless mission to transform lives through education. Shri Jethmalani's sentiments capture the essence of KISS as more than just an institution—it is a movement driven by compassion, humility, and an unwavering commitment to uplifting society's most vulnerable.

Dr. S. C. Jamir
His Excellency the Governor of Odisha
His admiration for the unparalleled contribution of Kalinga Institute of Social Sciences (KISS), stating,
"I have found enough reasons to cheer about for obvious reasons. No other organization can match the facility that KISS provides to its students."

These powerful words emphasize the exceptional infrastructure and support system that KISS offers, ensuring that every student receives not just education but holistic care and empowerment. Under the visionary leadership of Dr. Achyuta Samanta, KISS has set a global benchmark in providing comprehensive facilities that cater to the academic, cultural, and personal growth of its students. Dr. Jamir's recognition highlights the uniqueness of KISS as a transformative institution that empowers marginalized communities, equipping them to lead lives of dignity and purpose.

Prof. Ved Prakash
Hon'ble Chairman of University Grants Commission (UGC)

He offered profound recognition of the extraordinary work at Kalinga Institute of Social Sciences (KISS). Reflecting on his visit, he remarked,
"When you go to KISS, you witness a university that stands for humanity. When thousands of children are eating together, you see the true elements of humanism on the campus. Such a vision requires commitment of the highest order, passion—almost close to obsession. Only then can one bring about this kind of qualitative change."

As the head of the apex body for higher education in India, Prof. Prakash's words carry immense significance. His acknowledgment of KISS as a model of humanism and transformative education underscores the institution's unique role in redefining education for marginalized communities. Under the leadership of Dr. Achyuta Samanta, KISS has seamlessly integrated academic excellence with a profound commitment to humanity, fostering a culture of inclusion, compassion, and empowerment. Prof. Prakash's admiration highlights KISS as not just an institution but a movement that inspires the world by demonstrating how education can create a more equitable and humane society.

Dr. Raghuram Rajan,
Hon'ble Governor of the Reserve Bank of India

One of the world's most renowned economists, shared his awe and admiration after witnessing the extraordinary model of Kalinga Institute of Social Sciences (KISS). He remarked,
"What I have seen in KISS was beyond my wildest

imaginations; I am astonished to witness KISS' unique financial model of providing free education to 25,000 poor tribal children."

As an economist, Dr. Rajan's acknowledgment highlights the innovative and sustainable financial framework of KISS, which operates without government funding, relying instead on cross-subsidization from its sister institution, KIIT. This groundbreaking model is a testament to the vision and ingenuity of Dr. Achyuta Samanta, who has successfully combined education, empowerment, and sustainability to create a self-reliant institution. Dr. Rajan's recognition underscores the significance of KISS as not only an educational institution but also a pioneering economic model that demonstrates how strategic planning and compassionate leadership can drive transformative social change at scale.

Shri Jual Oram
Hon'ble Minister for Tribal Affairs

He shared his heartfelt connection with Kalinga Institute of Social Sciences (KISS), stating,
"I have been to KISS on many occasions, but the more I visit KISS, I feel I am at home. Dr. Samanta is a living legend."

These words reflect Shri Oram's deep admiration for the unique environment of inclusivity and compassion that KISS fosters. His recognition of Dr. Achyuta Samanta as a "living legend" highlights the remarkable contributions of a visionary leader who has dedicated his life to empowering marginalized tribal communities through holistic education. Shri Oram's sentiments underscore how KISS has become not just an institution but a sanctuary of hope, dignity, and opportunity, embodying the true spirit of humanity and social transformation.

Shri Naveen Patnaik
Hon'ble Former Chief Minister of Odisha

He expressed his deep appreciation for the transformative work of Kalinga Institute of Social Sciences (KISS), stating,
"KISS has gained a good reputation in the country. I pray for further progress and growth of Kalinga Institute of Social Sciences (KISS)."

These words reflect the Chief Minister's

acknowledgment of KISS as a pioneering institution that has set new standards in education, particularly in uplifting marginalized communities. Under the visionary leadership of Dr. Achyuta Samanta, KISS has not only earned national recognition but has also become a model for holistic education that integrates academic excellence with social empowerment. Shri Patnaik's blessings and prayers for the institution's continued progress emphasize the vital role KISS plays in shaping the future of tribal children and contributing to the broader socio-economic development of the nation.

Prof. Ganeshi Lal
Hon'ble former Governor of Odisha,

He spoke with deep reverence about the remarkable work of Kalinga Institute of Social Sciences (KISS) and its founder, Dr. Achyuta Samanta. He remarked,
"KIIT & KISS are divine creations through Prof. Samanta. He is bringing smiles to underprivileged children. He is loving those who have never been loved before. Therefore, I regard him as an alien."

These powerful words reflect the extraordinary impact of Dr. Samanta's work in transforming the lives of marginalized children. Prof. Lal's reference to Dr. Samanta as "an alien" underscores the profound and otherworldly nature of his compassion and selfless dedication to humanity. Through KISS, Dr. Samanta has not only created an institution but a movement, where love, care, and education meet to uplift the most vulnerable. His unwavering commitment to providing opportunities for those who have been overlooked and neglected makes him a beacon of hope and a true humanitarian in the modern world.

Spiritual Leaders

The Kalinga Institute of Social Sciences (KISS) has not only garnered recognition as a center for academic excellence and social empowerment but also as a hub of holistic education rooted in values of compassion, inclusivity, and service. Esteemed spiritual leaders from around the world have lauded KISS for its transformative impact on marginalized communities, acknowledging its role in nurturing humanity's collective spirit. Their heartfelt words of admiration reflect the profound alignment between KISS's mission and the universal values of love, harmony, and empowerment.

His Holiness the 14th Dalai Lama

His Holiness the 14th Dalai Lama, a global symbol of compassion and peace, expressed profound admiration for Dr. Achyuta Samanta during his visit to Kalinga Institute of Social Sciences (KISS). He remarked,

"Dr. Samanta is a great humanitarian who loves people and truly deserves to receive a humanitarian award himself. I am deeply honored to receive the 10th KISS Humanitarian Award from him. For me, this prize is no less than the Nobel Prize."

These words from His Holiness, a Nobel Laureate himself, elevate the global stature of KISS and its visionary founder. The Dalai Lama's acknowledgment of Dr. Samanta's unparalleled dedication to humanity underscores his exceptional contributions to education, empowerment, and social equity. The award ceremony not only recognized the Dalai Lama's lifelong pursuit of compassion and peace but also reflected the shared ethos of KISS as a beacon of hope and transformation for the underprivileged. His Holiness's reverence for Dr. Samanta reinforces the universal impact of KISS in redefining holistic education and serving as an instrument of global change.

Minister of Religion, Brahmarishi Mission, UK (2023)

During her visit to Kalinga Institute of Social Sciences (KISS) in 2023, the Minister of Religion from the Brahmarishi Mission, UK, expressed her profound admiration for the institution. She remarked:

"At KISS, I feel that the Universe wants me here. This is the wonder. Samanta ji, you are an ideal for politicians, social workers, and religious leaders. KISS is a Karmabhoomi."

Her words reflected KISS's transformative impact on global visitors and emphasized its role as a beacon of education and social service.

Sri Mata Amritanandamayi Devi (Amma)
Spiritual Leader, Guru, and Humanitarian

Sri Mata Amritanandamayi Devi, widely revered for her spiritual teachings and humanitarian endeavors, lauded the efforts of Prof. Achyuta Samanta and the mission of KISS. She stated:
"The most important thing to be developed through education is compassion towards our fellow beings. I heartily applaud Prof. Achyuta Samanta as he has chosen to offer his humanitarian service."

Her words reflect the profound alignment between her spiritual philosophy and the transformative work undertaken by KISS, emphasizing compassion as the cornerstone of true education.

His Holiness Gyetrul Jigme Rinpoche
Master of Tibetan Buddhism and Spiritual Director of the Ripa International Center

During his visits to KISS, His Holiness Gyetrul Jigme Rinpoche expressed his deep admiration for the institution and its mission. He remarked:
"I have been profoundly touched during my visits to KISS, and I get a feeling that the voice of the tribal community of India is here."

His statement highlights the pivotal role KISS plays in empowering and representing tribal communities, resonating deeply with his teachings of compassion and service.

His Holiness Swami Sarvapriyananda
Minister & Spiritual Leader of the Vedanta Society of New York

During his visit to the remarkable campuses of KIIT and the Kalinga Institute of Social Sciences (KISS), His Holiness Swami Sarvapriyananda shared his profound admiration. He observed:
"While going around the wonderful campuses of KIIT and Kalinga Institute of Social Sciences (KISS) this morning, my feeling was that while Harvard, a great

university and one of the best in the world, is the present, this is the future."

His Holiness's words resonate with the visionary work of these institutions, recognizing their potential to shape the future of education and societal transformation on a global scale.

Celebrities

Dr. Ricky G. Kej
Internationally renowned Indian music composer and three-time Grammy Award winner
He highlighted the power of small changes in driving significant transformation.
"The biggest roadblock we face today is the thought that someone else will make a difference. However, small incremental changes can lead to a transformative impact, as exemplified by KISS."

Rooted in the educational philosophy of Achyuta Samanta, KISS stands as a beacon of holistic education, empowering marginalized communities through knowledge, values, and self-reliance. It demonstrates how consistent efforts in education can break the cycle of poverty and create lasting societal change.

Mr. Rahul Bose
President of Rugby India, acknowledged the significant role of KIIT and KISS in the growth of rugby in the country.
"KIIT and KISS are the home of Rugby in India."
KISS, founded on the philosophy of holistic education envisioned by Achyuta Samanta, integrates academics, sports, and skill development to create well-rounded individuals. The institution not only provides quality education to tribal students but also nurtures their talents in various fields, with sports being a key component. Rugby, along with other disciplines, has flourished at KISS, proving that a holistic approach to education empowers students to excel beyond academics, fostering discipline, teamwork, and resilience—essential qualities for success in life.

Shri Amitabh Bachchan
Noted Film Actor, Director and Producer

Shri Amitabh Bachchan, renowned film actor, director, and producer, expressed deep appreciation for the transformative impact of KISS in uplifting marginalized communities.

"I was really enthused by the steps taken by you (Achyuta Samanta) in eradicating poverty through imparting quality education to the tribal children and thereby ensuring sustainable livelihood to them. I am moved by the exemplary work carried out by you."

KISS stands as a testament to the power of holistic education in breaking the cycle of poverty. Under the visionary leadership of Achyuta Samanta, the institution goes beyond academics, equipping tribal children with the knowledge, skills, and values necessary for a sustainable livelihood. By integrating education with skill development, sports, and cultural preservation, KISS ensures that every student is empowered to lead a dignified and self-reliant life, reinforcing the idea that true societal transformation begins with inclusive and quality education.

Smt. Vidya Balan
Noted Film Actor, Director and Producer

She emphasized the transformative power of education and lauded the remarkable efforts of Achyuta Samanta through KISS.

"To educate is to change a life forever. Today, Dr. Samanta provides free education, meals, boarding, and lodging to over 25,000 students. There are very few Samantas in India and even fewer whose efforts get recognized. It is time for India to recognize and produce even more Samantas."

Her words exemplify how holistic education can drive social change by empowering marginalized communities with knowledge, skills, and opportunities. Achyuta Samanta's vision ensures that tribal children receive not just education but also the necessary support to lead dignified and self-sufficient lives. His model of free, inclusive, and value-based education proves that transformative leadership in education can uplift generations and shape a more equitable society.

Ms. Ashley Judd
Noted American Actress, UNFPA Goodwill Ambassador

Ms. Ashley Judd applauded the transformative impact of KISS in breaking the cycle of poverty through education and holistic support.

"KISS is transforming poverty through education and nutrition. This award will empower and make me energetic to do more work for women and girl children. Support each other, help your people and your community."

KISS, driven by the visionary leadership of Achyuta Samanta, stands as a global model of holistic education that uplifts marginalized communities. By providing not only free education but also nutrition, healthcare, and skill development, KISS ensures that every child—especially girls—gets the opportunity to thrive. The institution's unwavering commitment to empowerment aligns with the broader mission of creating a more equitable and inclusive society, where education becomes the most powerful tool for lasting transformation.

Padma Bhushan A.R. Rahman
*Noted **Oscar Winning Music Composer***

He praised the transformative impact of KISS and underscored the need to replicate its model for national progress.

"The Kalinga Institute of Social Sciences University is a residential tribal school. I think people like him have to be replicated. This institution (KISS) has to be replicated in every village, every city, every state. That would be the progress for the country."

His words highlight the far-reaching significance of KISS, which stands as a beacon of holistic education and social transformation. Under the leadership of Achyuta Samanta, KISS has pioneered an inclusive model that integrates quality education, nutrition, and skill development for marginalized communities. The success of this institution proves that replicating such initiatives across the nation can drive true progress, ensuring a future where education empowers and uplifts every child, regardless of background.

Closing Note

The voices of these eminent personalities reaffirm a fundamental truth—education is not just about literacy, but about transformation. Their words celebrate the holistic educational model of KISS, which blends academic learning, skill development, values, and self-reliance.

From former Presidents and Prime Ministers to Nobel Laureates and global changemakers, these leaders recognize that true education must go beyond textbooks. KISS has redefined learning by fostering an environment where underprivileged children are not just taught, but empowered to dream, lead, and uplift society.

As Dr. A.P.J. Abdul Kalam envisioned, education must build a nation of thinkers and doers, and Prof. Achyuta Samanta's holistic approach to education is a living example of that vision. Prime Minister Narendra Modi, Dalai Lama, and other world leaders have acknowledged that KISS is not just an institution—it is a movement of change, a model for inclusive and sustainable education.

In a world striving for equality and social justice, holistic education is the key to eradicating poverty, fostering peace, and driving sustainable development. KISS embodies this philosophy, proving that when education is holistic, it can create not just scholars, but compassionate, skilled, and responsible global citizens.

As you turn the pages of this book, may you find inspiration in this transformative vision and realize that education, when redefined holistically, is the greatest force for social change.

KISS at a Glance

The following features and highlights have earned KISS (Kalinga Institute of Social Sciences) worldwide recognition:

1. Accommodates more than 30,000 tribal students, from the poorest of the poor.
2. KISS provides free accommodation, food, healthcare, education, and vocational training, along with yoga, sports and games, life skills, and spiritual and aesthetic education, ensuring holistic development for all its students.
3. Holds special consultative status with the United Nations (UN).
4. Recognized as the world's largest residential institute by the Limca Book of Records.
5. A center of global attraction and interest.
6. Spans over 84 acres of land.
7. Boasts a built-up area of more than Near about 20 lakh (2 Million) square feet.
8. Offers education from kindergarten (KG) to Ph.D. within a single campus.
9. Considered the heart of tribal communities worldwide.
10. Regarded as a man-made wonder by many across the globe.
11. Features a dedicated Tribal Museum.

12. Operates a fully mechanized kitchen system.
13. Provides a Wi-Fi-enabled campus.
14. Includes digital classrooms for modern learning.
15. Has a massive dining hall where more than 5,000 students can dine simultaneously.
16. Hosts a huge meeting space accommodating 30,000 students.
17. Offers a state-of-the-art sports complex for multi-disciplinary sports activities.
18. Houses more than ten hostels for students.
19. Provides separate staff quarters.
20. Maintains a 100-bed dispensary for immediate healthcare needs.
21. Features a miniature replica of the Puri Jagannath Temple for spiritual development.
22. Operates five laptop labs with internet access to ensure computer education for all.
23. Recognized as one of the cleanest and most hygienic campuses.
24. Includes a Botanical Garden and Science Park.
25. Provides dedicated fields for various sports.
26. Functions with over 20 committees to manage all campus activities.
27. Hosts a graceful and grand Chariot Festival, uniquely celebrated and renowned across Odisha, second only to the famous Puri Rath Yatra.

28. Has a vast library with over 40,000 titles.
29. Employs more than 1,000 teaching staff.
30. Operates a dedicated research wing to promote higher studies and tribal-focused research.
31. KISS offers eco-friendly shuttle services and vehicles powered by green technologies such as solar energy and battery systems, ensuring zero CO_2 emissions within the campus.
32. Maintains a separate Board of Studies to oversee academic activities and student progress year-round.
33. Provides 24x7 mechanized care for students.
34. Runs a large vocational wing to empower students with self-sufficiency and contribute to campus upkeep.
35. Includes a dedicated placement cell to facilitate student employment.
36. Operates a Directorate of Guidance and Counseling to support students in various aspects.
37. Features an extensive gallery of tribal art and crafts to promote tribal culture and generate financial benefits for students.
38. Serves as the world's best tribal residential model, succeeding where other models have failed.
39. Maintains MOUs with multiple government and non-government organizations for academic development and student placements.
40. Focuses on both tribal and women empowerment.
41. Ensures gender balance, with 60% of students being girls and 40% boys.

Prof. Achyuta Samanta
(1965-Serving)

"The woods are lovely, dark and deep,
but I have promises to keep,
and miles to go before I sleep,
and miles to go before I sleep."

ସୁନ୍ଦର ଯେତିକି ଅନ୍ଧାର ସେତିକି...
ଏହି ଯେ ଗହନ ବନ।
ତେଣୁ ତୁ ଆପଣା ସଙ୍କଳ୍ପେ ଅଟଳ...
ଅଚଳ ରହରେ ମନ।
ଆଗରେ ପଡ଼ିଛି ପଥ ବହୁଦୂର...
ଆହୁରି କେତେ ଯେ ବାକି।
ଚାଲିବି ଚାଲିବି ନ ପଡ଼ିବି ଥକି...
ମୁଦିବା ଆଗରୁ ଆଖି... ମୁଦିବା ଆଗରୁ ଆଖି... ମୁଦିବା ଆଗରୁ ଆଖି...

— From "Stopping by Woods on a Snowy Evening" by Robert Frost

The 21st century is marked by *globalization*, an era where the development of nations hinges on the integration of economies and societies. This integration is facilitated by the cross-border flow of information, ideas, technologies, goods, services, capital, finance, and people. In such a dynamic and interconnected world, a well-educated workforce equipped with modern skills is not just desirable but essential. Only such a workforce can effectively compete and thrive in the opportunities brought about by globalization.

In this global landscape, education plays a pivotal role in national development. Thinkers and policymakers alike have long emphasized education as a powerful tool for reducing poverty, fostering economic growth, and building a skilled workforce capable of competing in an increasingly competitive global economy. It is an indispensable asset for any nation seeking progress and prosperity.

One visionary who has championed this philosophy of education is **Prof. Achyuta Samanta**, a progressive educational entrepreneur and a trailblazer in the field of holistic learning. His journey reflects the transformative power of education, shaped by the challenging circumstances and compulsions of his own life. Driven by a deep understanding of societal needs and a commitment to uplifting marginalized communities, Prof. Samanta has evolved a unique ideology of education that addresses the specific needs of India and resonates globally.

This philosophy, known as **Holistic Education**, goes beyond conventional methods. It encompasses the "whole" view of education, addressing not only intellectual development but also emotional, social, ethical, and physical growth. Holistic Education, as envisioned by Prof. Samanta, is a beacon of hope and a revolutionary concept, especially for the tribal communities across the globe.

Prof. Samanta's approach has significantly impacted educational practices in both the 20th and 21st centuries. His work underscores the importance of integrating practical skills, cultural preservation, and values-based education into a unified framework. By tailoring education to meet the demands of a globalized world while addressing the unique challenges of local communities, he has demonstrated that education can serve as a powerful catalyst for social transformation.

In essence, Holistic Education is not just a teaching philosophy—it is a *gift* to the world, a legacy that underscores the critical role of education in empowering individuals and communities to thrive in an interconnected, globalized era. Prof. Samanta's vision continues to inspire efforts to create an equitable, inclusive, and progressive global society.

Brief Sketch of Life History

Professor Achyuta Samanta's life is an extraordinary journey from hardship to global recognition, defined by resilience and a deep commitment to transforming lives through education. Born in 1965 in the village of Kalarabanka, located in Odisha's Cuttack District, he was the youngest of seven siblings in a family that faced extreme poverty. His father, Shri Anadi Charan Samanta, passed away when Achyuta was just four years old, leaving his widowed mother, Smt. Nilima Rani Samanta, to raise the family amidst immense financial and social challenges.

It is the story of a man who rose from stark poverty to not only transform

Prof. Achyuta Samanta with his beloved mother — the source of his inspiration and values.

---

his own life but also positively impact the lives of thousands through the power of education. Prof. Achyuta Samanta, an educational entrepreneur, is the visionary founder of the Kalinga Institute of Social Sciences (KISS), the largest tribal educational institution in the world. Based in Odisha, KISS has grown to serve as a beacon of hope and empowerment for tribal communities, extending its impact globally. Prof. Samanta's journey is among the most inspiring stories of modern India, exemplifying how resilience, vision, and education can drive transformative change.

Achyuta Samanta's pursuit of education, against all odds, is a tale of remarkable perseverance and determination. Growing up in dire poverty, education seemed an unattainable dream for a boy from a small, underprivileged village. Yet, driven by an innate instinct and an unyielding will, young Samanta made the courageous decision to follow a group of older boys to school, a move that would change the course of his life forever.

Initially, his presence in the classroom surprised even the headmaster, who was eventually moved by Samanta's resolve and allowed him to stay. This marked the beginning of a challenging yet inspiring journey. From primary school to high school, then to college, and eventually to the university, Achyuta's education was a story of relentless effort and brilliance, supported by merit scholarships at every step.

Transitioning from his rural village to a district headquarters and later to the state capital, Achyuta experienced the harsh realities of life. Hunger and financial constraints were constant companions, but they never deterred him. Even in the face of extreme hardship, he managed to earn a Master's degree in Chemistry from Utkal University. The meager scholarships he received were insufficient, and to make ends meet, he began tutoring students, balancing his academic pursuits with his need to support himself and his family.

These adversities forged his character, turning his struggles into stepping stones. Achyuta Samanta's ability to convert the challenges of his life into opportunities for growth set him apart. His academic excellence eventually led to a teaching position at a local college, a stable job that allowed him to assist his family. However, his destiny had far greater plans.

This phase of his life laid the foundation for his later achievements as an educational entrepreneur and philanthropist. The values he learned from his struggles—resilience, empathy, and an unwavering commitment to education—would become the guiding principles of his mission to uplift the underprivileged through holistic education.

His struggling life History to present Legend (as an educational entrepreneur)

One early morning in 1965, at around 5:00 a.m., a four-year-old boy woke to an atmosphere of despair and confusion. He could not comprehend why his family members were crying inconsolably, their faces reflecting deep sorrow. The child, too young to grasp the concept of death, looked around for answers. Slowly, he came to understand that his father had passed away in a tragic train accident.

The loss plunged the family into a state of utter devastation. The deceased father had been a humble worker in an industry, and his untimely death left behind a widowed wife and seven children, the youngest just a month old and the eldest only 17. With no savings or financial resources to rely on, the family faced an uncertain and daunting future. This marked the beginning of a life filled with challenges for the young boy, one that would shape his extraordinary journey of resilience and achievement.

The siblings, including the young boy, grew up in the grip of extreme poverty in a remote village in Odisha, India. From a tender age, the boy took it upon himself to support his widowed mother, voluntarily performing various menial tasks to contribute to the family's survival. Forced by circumstances, he quickly learned to navigate life's hardships and became self-reliant by the age of five. These early struggles forged his resilience and shaped his determination to overcome adversity, laying the foundation for his self-made journey and remarkable future.

He was a child wise beyond his years, bearing responsibilities far beyond his tender age. He comforted his grieving mother by wiping her tears and offered his lap as a place of solace for his little sister to sleep. By the age of seven, he was already showing an extraordinary spirit of generosity. Whatever little he earned from his menial jobs, he shared with his classmates, setting aside one rupee from his day's wages to treat his four friends to tea and snacks at a nearby shop.

Even as a child, his compassion extended beyond his immediate circle. He selflessly helped the villagers, often using his time and energy to fetch groceries and provisions for them from the nearby market.

As he grew older and entered adulthood, his innate kindness only deepened. While pursuing his Master's degree at Utkal University in Bhubaneswar, he displayed an act of selflessness that epitomized his character. When his eldest brother gave him 300 rupees to attend a college picnic, he quietly handed the money to a friend who couldn't afford to join. Watching his friend enjoy the outing brought him more happiness than participating himself.

These small but profound gestures of kindness reflected a heart rich with empathy, even amidst personal deprivation. They were glimpses of the man he would become—a visionary who would transform the lives of countless others through his unwavering compassion and commitment to service.

After completing his Master's degree in Chemistry, the young man secured a teaching position at a local college. Despite the modest nature of his job, he began tutoring privately to supplement his income. However, instead of indulging in personal comforts, he used his earnings selflessly to support his impoverished family and assist friends in need. For a decade (1987–1997), his life was a testament to sacrifice, as he prioritized the well-being of others over his own.

Earning respect in a world that often values material success over moral integrity is a formidable challenge. Sustaining that respect through unwavering principles is an even rarer feat. Much like how Rabindranath Tagore's conferral of the title "Mahatma" upon Mohandas Karamchand Gandhi in the 1930s resonated deeply with millions in the Indian subcontinent, this young man's selflessness and dedication to humanity left an indelible mark on the hearts of those around him. His actions embodied an ideology rooted in compassion, service, and humility—values destined to inspire and endure for generations, much like the legacy of the Mahatma.

Near about four decades ago, a young village boy, Achyuta Samanta, arrived in the temple city of Bhubaneswar with no clear direction or resources to climb the social ladder. Life seemed uncertain, but what began as a journey without a roadmap soon transformed into an extraordinary saga of vision and perseverance. Amid the corridors of Odisha's political landscape—often dominated by lofty promises—Samanta envisioned a dream not for personal power but for the upliftment of the marginalized. His dream was one of service, born out of an unyielding commitment to sacrifice for a cause larger than himself.

Through sheer determination and relentless effort, he carved a path for himself, starting as a teacher. For his students, he became not just an educator but a guide, mentor, and inspiration—earning the endearing title "SAMANTA SIR." While others sought comfort and luxury, Samanta dedicated his prime years to an impossible mission: transforming the lives of the poorest of the poor.

The price of his vision was immense. Sacrificing personal time, luxury, and leisure, he poured everything into his cause, enduring unimaginable social and economic challenges. Yet, these sacrifices gave birth to KISS (Kalinga Institute of Social Sciences)—a beacon of hope for tribal communities, not just in Odisha but across the globe. Today, KISS stands as a testament to his selflessness, reflecting his unwavering belief in education as the tool to transform lives.

Samanta's journey is not just the story of an institution; it is the story of a man whose sacrifices have placed him in the hearts of millions. He may have started with nothing, but his life's work has made him a global figure, a name synonymous with hope and humanity. The title "Sir Samanta" is more than a recognition; it is the embodiment of his vision to light up the lives of the most disadvantaged and rewrite their destiny through education.

In today's world, we often pursue goals that rely heavily on the advancements of science and technology, sometimes at the cost of our freedom and humanity. Yet, the plight of the poor and marginalized—the "have-nots" that Karl Marx so poignantly described—remains a glaring issue. These communities, particularly the downtrodden tribal populations, have historically been subjected to systemic social and economic oppression, leaving them struggling to survive, let alone thrive.

In this landscape of inequality, Prof. Achyuta Samanta stands as a beacon of hope. Against all odds, he has dedicated his life to uplifting tribal communities, striving to bring smiles to faces that had forgotten the meaning of joy. His efforts go beyond mere alleviation of poverty; they focus on integration—bringing the tribal population *"together with the mainstream."* This vision transcends the tribal ordinary, as seen in KISS (Kalinga Institute of Social Sciences), an institution recognized globally, even by the United Nations, for its transformative impact. KISS has also nurtured budding athletes who now make their mark in international sports arenas, creating a sense of pride and identity for communities once overlooked.

Prof. Samanta's approach extends beyond education. He understands that the path to empowerment lies in providing sustainable livelihoods. In a world where social status is often dictated by economic success, he emphasizes the importance of quality education as a foundation for survival and growth. His visionary model at KISS offers education from kindergarten to postgraduate and doctoral levels, creating a continuum of opportunities for tribal students. Through his guidance, these students are taught to reflect on their journey with the thought: *"What you had, what you have, and what you will have."*

Samanta's unwavering commitment to fostering self-reliance, coupled with his emphasis on dignity and inclusion, is reshaping the narrative for tribal communities. His work reminds us that true progress lies not just in technological achievements but in uplifting those at the margins of society and ensuring that everyone has the opportunity to smile, dream, and succeed.

Vision

Prof. Achyuta Samanta envisions KISS (Kalinga Institute of Social Sciences) as a transformative center of education, dedicated to empowering the poorest of the poor among tribal communities. His mission is to provide these marginalized sections with access to quality formal education, fostering sustainable livelihoods while promoting all-round development. This vision goes beyond education—it aims to integrate tribal youth into the global mainstream with dignity and opportunity.

Social Arena
Prof. Samanta's dedication to social upliftment is exemplified in his impactful initiatives:

1. **Empowering Communities:**
   He has touched the lives of over 2 million people through education and skill development, in partnership with UNFPA. His "New Mind, New Dream Programme" (*Nua Mana Nua Sapana*) reaches across 30 districts of Odisha, benefiting 17,000 villages and fostering hope and self-reliance among the underprivileged.
2. **KAMPASHN Initiative:**
   As part of his unwavering commitment to social welfare, Prof. Samanta launched KAMPASHN, a charitable store for distributing used garments and other essential items to those in need, reinforcing the importance of sharing and compassion.
3. **Philosophy of Life – The Art of Giving:**
   At the heart of his endeavors lies the *Art of Giving,* a philosophy that encourages generosity and selflessness as pathways to inner peace. This movement has gained global recognition, uniting individuals in the spirit of altruism.
4. **Art of Appreciation:**
   Prof. Samanta propagates the *Art of Appreciation*, inspiring people to cultivate gratitude, recognize others' contributions, and embrace positivity.
5. **India Against Negativity:**
   Through his *India Against Negativity* campaign, Prof. Samanta aspires to eradicate the destructive mindset of pessimism, replacing it with optimism and proactive engagement.

Impact

Prof. Samanta's visionary leadership has reshaped the landscape for the marginalized, combining education, social empowerment, and human values. His innovative initiatives exemplify how a single individual, driven by compassion and determination, can create ripples of change, transforming countless lives and leaving an indelible mark on humanity.

Great Achievements & KISS

Prof. Achyuta Samanta's life story is not only one of personal triumph over adversity but also a testament to the power of vision, perseverance, and selflessness. **His 'brainchild', KISS** (Kalinga Institute of Social Sciences),

stands as a beacon of hope for tribal communities across India and the globe. It is a recognition of his relentless efforts to uplift the marginalized through education, ensuring that they are not only educated but empowered to change their own destinies. Although KISS was born out of humble means, it has become a globally recognized institution, with special recognition from the United Nations (UN). This acknowledgment speaks volumes about Prof. Samanta's vision and the immense impact his work has had on society.

A man of many talents and an unwavering commitment to humanity, Prof. Samanta's contributions have been acknowledged by both national and international organizations. His work has earned him numerous honors, memberships, and awards, solidifying his position as one of the most influential figures in modern India. Below are some of his key recognitions:

1. United Nations Recognition:

UN Special Status for KISS:
The United Nations has provided special recognition to KISS for its efforts in advancing education and empowerment for tribal populations. KISS has been recognized for its role in contributing to the Sustainable Development Goals (SDGs), especially those related to education (SDG 4) and inequality (SDG 10). The UN's endorsement highlights the institution's ability to provide free,

quality education to over 30,000 tribal students, empowering them to break the cycle of poverty.

In addition, Prof. Samanta's philosophy of holistic education, focusing on tribal development, received a warm reception at various UN forums, where KISS was highlighted as a model of inclusive education.

2. National Recognition:

Prof. Samanta has received numerous accolades from the Government of India for his dedication to social welfare and educational reform. His efforts to bring tribal youth into the mainstream of education have garnered national praise, positioning him as a pioneer in the field of education and social entrepreneurship.

Rashtriya Bal Kalyan Award:
- In 2014, Prof. Samanta was honored with the Rashtriya Bal Kalyan Award by the Ministry of Women and Child Development, Government of India, in recognition of his contributions to child welfare and development, particularly through the KISS and KIIT initiatives. The award acknowledged his outstanding work in empowering children from the poorest backgrounds and offering them opportunities for holistic growth.

National Award for Excellence in Education:
- The President of India also awarded Prof. Samanta the National Award for Excellence in Education for his innovative approach to tribal education and his ability to create an inclusive educational environment that fosters the all-round development of students from economically disadvantaged backgrounds.

3. International Recognition:

His work has also earned him accolades from various international organizations, reinforcing his stature as a global leader in the field of education and social empowerment. These recognitions are a testament to his universal approach to solving the challenges faced by marginalized communities.

UNESCO and UNICEF Partnerships:
- Prof. Samanta has been recognized by international organizations such as UNESCO and UNICEF for his role in improving educational access for disadvantaged tribal communities. His approach to education has been considered an exemplar of global best practices, particularly in terms of inclusivity, sustainability, and community-based development.
- Under his leadership, KISS was able to collaborate with UNICEF on various projects aimed at promoting quality education, child welfare, and gender equality.

Global Recognition for KISS's Education Model:
- KISS's unique educational model, which provides free education from kindergarten to post-graduate levels, has gained international recognition. The institution's emphasis on both formal and informal education, along with its focus on skill development and sports, has been highlighted by global media, including BBC and The Times of India. KISS has become a benchmark for inclusive education globally.

Recognition by the European Parliament:
- Prof. Samanta was invited to speak at the European Parliament on his work with tribal communities and the transformative impact of KISS. He has been praised for his ability to integrate education with social entrepreneurship, and his work has been cited as a global example of how to uplift marginalized communities through quality education.

4. Honours and Awards:
Prof. Samanta has been conferred with several honorary titles, including "Doctor of Letters" and "Doctor of Science," in recognition of his exceptional contributions to education and social service. These honors are not only a personal achievement but also a recognition of the transformative impact he has had on thousands of lives.

Honorary Doctorates:
- Prof. Samanta has been awarded multiple honorary doctorates (D.Litt and D.Sc) by prestigious universities around the world. These honors are a recognition of his groundbreaking work in the fields of

education, social entrepreneurship, and community development. He has received honorary degrees from institutions like Utkal University and other global universities.

Global Social Entrepreneurship Award:
- Prof. Samanta received the prestigious **Global Social Entrepreneurship Award** for his innovative approach to social change through education. This award recognized his efforts in creating sustainable educational models that not only focus on academic success but also on holistic development, including sports, life skills, and personal growth.

The Times of India Social Impact Award:
- In 2018, Prof. Samanta received the **Times of India Social Impact Award** for his lifelong dedication to transforming the lives of tribal communities in Odisha and beyond. His pioneering work with KISS was celebrated as one of the most impactful educational initiatives in India.

5. Memberships and Associations:
As a man of many roles, Prof. Samanta holds several prestigious memberships, including affiliations with various academic and social organizations. His leadership in these circles further amplifies his ability to bring about meaningful change, not just in India but globally.

Member, UN Global Compact (UNGC):
- Prof. Samanta is a member of the **United Nations Global Compact**, a voluntary initiative to implement sustainable and socially responsible policies. As a member, he promotes the principles of human rights, social justice, and sustainable development, aligning with the global goals set by the UN.

Member, Global Philanthropy Alliance (GPA):
- Prof. Samanta is an active member of the **Global Philanthropy Alliance**, where he collaborates with global leaders, organizations, and governments to enhance philanthropic initiatives, especially those focused on education, healthcare, and social development for marginalized communities.

Board Member, UNESCO's International Institute for Capacity Building in Africa (IICBA):

- Prof. Samanta is on the board of the **International Institute for Capacity Building in Africa**, where he plays a crucial role in shaping educational strategies to help African nations improve their education systems, particularly in rural and underprivileged areas.

Association with Commonwealth of Learning (COL):

- Prof. Samanta's work in inclusive education has earned him a place within the **Commonwealth of Learning (COL)**, a global organization dedicated to promoting learning for sustainable development. He shares his expertise with global educators to promote quality education for all.

Member, International Council for Education and Development (ICED):

- Prof. Samanta is a member of the **International Council for Education and Development**, where he contributes his knowledge and experience on how to integrate education with social entrepreneurship for long-term sustainability.

Prof. Samanta's story is a living example of how one person, through sheer dedication and an unwavering belief in the power of education, can change the lives of countless others. His achievements are not just a reflection of personal success but are a beacon of hope for millions of tribal people who now see a brighter future ahead.

National Recognition as a Member

Position/Role	Organization/Committee	Duration	Affiliation
Member	University Grants Commission (UGC)	2008-2014	Ministry of HRD, Government of India
Member	Executive Committee, All India Council for Technical Education (AICTE)	N/A	Ministry of HRD, Government of India
President's Nominee	Academic Council, Assam Central University	N/A	President of India
Nominee	Academic Council, Central University, Odisha	N/A	Ministry of HRD, Govt. of India
Member	MHRD Committee on 'Round Table' on Disadvantaged Sections, Women, and SC/ST	N/A	MHRD, Govt. of India
Member	High-Level Committee on Higher Education, Planning Commission	N/A	Government of India

Position/Role	Organization/Committee	Duration	Affiliation
Member	MOEF Committee on Forest Rights Act	N/A	Ministry of Environment & Forest, Tribal Affairs, Govt. of India
Member	General Body, CAPART (Centre for Advancement of People's Action and Rural Technology)	N/A	Govt. of India
Member	Executive Committee, Indian Red Cross Society, Odisha State Branch	N/A	Governor's Nominee
Vice-President	Bharat Scouts & Guides, Odisha	N/A	-

National Recognition as a Serving Member

Position/Role	Organization/Committee	Affiliation
Member	National Council for Teacher Education (NCTE)	Ministry of HRD, India
Member	Coir Board, Kochi	Government of India

Position/Role	Organization/Committee	Affiliation
Member	National Executive Council, Indian Society for Technical Education (ISTE)	-
Member	Executive Committee, Indian Science Congress Association (ISCA), Kolkata	-
National Secretary	GGF Gandhi Global Family (GGF)	-

International Recognition as a Serving Member

Position/Role	Organization/Committee	Affiliation
Member	International Association of University Presidents (IAUP), U.S.A.	-
Member	International Institute of Education (IIE), New York	-
Member	Association of Universities of Asia Pacific (AUAP)	-

Position/Role	Organization/Committee	Affiliation
Member	University Mobility in Asia & the Pacific (UMAP), Bangkok (Thailand)	-
Member	Asia-Pacific Academic Consortium for Public Health (APACPH)	-
Member	United Nations Academic Impact (UNAI)	-
Member	Asia Economic Forum (AEF)	-

Recognition & Appreciation (Academics)

1. **GUSI Peace Prize International – 2014, Manila**
   Prof. Achyuta Samanta was honored with the prestigious GUSI Peace Prize in 2014 in recognition of his outstanding contributions to social development and the empowerment of underprivileged communities, especially through education.
2. **President's Gold Medal, International Association of Knowledge, Znanie, Moscow – 2014**
   Awarded the President's Gold Medal by the Znanie Association in Moscow for his exemplary leadership in advancing education and promoting global peace.
3. **Gold Medal for Outstanding Contribution in Education, Znanie, Moscow**
   Recognized for his profound impact on education, Prof. Samanta received a Gold Medal from the Znanie Association in Moscow, celebrating his commitment to transformative education systems.

4. **Highest Honour 'Goddess of Harvest OPS', Czech University of Life Sciences, Praha – 2013**
   In 2013, Prof. Samanta received the 'Goddess of Harvest OPS' honor from the Czech University of Life Sciences, Praha, for his significant contributions to education and social development.

Honoris Causa: D.Litt & D.Sc
(Doctor of Literature & Doctor of Science)

Prof. Achyuta Samanta has been conferred with multiple honorary doctorates by prestigious universities worldwide, recognizing his significant contributions to education, social development, and global peace. Below are the details of the institutions that honored him with the esteemed degrees of D.Litt. and D.Sc.:

- OIU, Colombo (2002 & 2005) – D.Sc.
- National University, Cambodia (2009)
- Hanseo University, South Korea (2010)
- Rashtriya Sanskrit Vidyapeetha - Central University, Tirupati, India (2011)
- National Formosa University, Taiwan (2012)
- Daffodil International University, Bangladesh (2014)
- International University of Kyrgyzstan (2014)
- The International School of Medicine, Bishkek, Kyrgyzstan (2014)
- Kainar University, Almaty, Kazakhstan (2014)
- Chosun University, South Korea (2014)
- Hangai University, Mongolia (2014)
- Soyol Erdem University, Mongolia (2014)
- Naryn State University, Kyrgyzstan (2014)
- Jalalabad State University, Kyrgyzstan (2014)
- Tabriz University, Iran (2014)
- Jalal-Abat State University (JASU), Kyrgyzstan (2014)
- Osh State University, Kyrgyzstan (2014)
- Modern University of Humanities, Moscow (2014)

These honorary doctorates are a testament to Prof. Samanta's global influence in the realm of education, his unrelenting pursuit of social justice, and his dedication to the betterment of underprivileged communities, particularly the tribal populations.

Record Book Achievements of Prof. Achyuta Samanta

Prof. Achyuta Samanta has achieved remarkable milestones that are recognized both nationally and internationally, making his journey an inspirational one. Below are some of his notable records:

- **Youngest Chancellor of Any University in India:**

Prof. Samanta became the youngest-ever Chancellor of a university in India, a position that reflects his outstanding leadership and vision for educational reform.

- **KIIT's Elevation to University in the Shortest Span of Time (6 years 7 months):**

Under his visionary leadership, KIIT (Kalinga Institute of Industrial Technology) achieved the remarkable feat of gaining university status in just 6 years and 7 months, making it one of the fastest-growing institutions in India.

- **Only Institution from ITI to Ph.D.:**

KIIT, under Prof. Samanta's guidance, became the only institution in India to offer a complete range of programs from ITI (Industrial Training Institute) to Ph.D., covering all academic levels and fields.

- **KISS - Largest Residential Institute for Tribal Children in the globe:**

KISS (Kalinga Institute of Social Sciences), founded by Prof. Samanta, is the largest residential institute in India dedicated to providing free education to tribal children, empowering them through holistic education and development programs.

These records not only highlight Prof. Samanta's exceptional accomplishments in the field of education but also his deep commitment to social justice, particularly the upliftment of tribal communities in India.

Recognition and Appreciation (Social Sector - National)

Prof. Achyuta Samanta's contributions to the social sector have been widely recognized both within India and globally. His relentless pursuit of social equity, particularly through the empowerment of marginalized communities, has earned him numerous prestigious awards and honors:

- National Young EDGE Award (2010)
- Asia's Best Social Entrepreneur, World HRD Congress, Singapore (2010)
- Godfrey Phillips Bravery Award (Social Bravery) - 2011
- Mahaveer Award, Bhagwan Mahaveer Foundation (2012)
- Jawaharlal Nehru Award (2012) – Awarded at the National Science Congress.
- Qimpro Platinum Standard Award (2011)
- Nominee - WISE Awards (2009) – Qatar Foundation.
- Gurudev Rabindranath Tagore Samman (2011)
- Dainik Bhaskar India Pride Award (2011) – For being a Change Agent in Social Development and Equity.
- Gandhi Seva Medal (2009) – For Philanthropy and Charity.
- Swami Vivekananda National Award (2010) – Government of Karnataka.
- Priya Odiya (Most Endeared Personality of Odisha) (2007) – A survey by a popular TV Channel.
- ICON of Odisha (2011) – Times of India.
- Humanitarian Award (2004) – Johannesburg, South Africa.
- Certificate of Excellence (2010) – Government of Cambodia.
- International Award, Certificate of Excellence (2010) – Muscat, Oman.
- Recognition from Social Entrepreneur, Skoll Foundation (2007) – One of the 15 best social entrepreneurs globally.
- Award of Excellence (2014) – Afro-Asian Book Council.
- Education Entrepreneur of the Year (2014) – ASSOCHAM.
- World of Difference Award (2013) – The International Alliance for Women (TIAW), USA.
- National Fellow Award (2014) – Computer Society of India.
- Dr. Pinnamaneni and Smt. Seetha Devi Foundation Award (2014)

In addition to these significant accolades, Prof. Samanta has received more than 200 state-level awards, reflecting the widespread recognition of his efforts in education, social work, and philanthropy. These awards underscore his unyielding commitment to bringing positive change to society, especially for the underprivileged and tribal communities, and resonate deeply with his core philosophy of social empowerment through education.

His Philosophy of Life: The Art of Giving

Prof. Achyuta Samanta's philosophy of life is rooted in the profound principle of the **"Art of Giving"**. This concept, which he has embraced since his childhood, has become the foundation of both his personal and professional life. Despite his monumental success and significant contributions to society, he lives a life of simplicity—residing in a modest two-room rented house, without personal possessions, and choosing to remain a bachelor. His only passion is bringing joy to the faces of thousands of underprivileged children, irrespective of caste, creed, or religion.

The **"Art of Giving"** has been an integral part of his existence, a philosophy he learned quietly in his early years and one that continues to guide him. He believes that the true purpose of life is to give without expecting anything in return. This practice, he argues, has the power to bring

peace to the human soul and foster harmony within society. Prof. Samanta's dedication to this cause led him to formally institutionalize the Art of Giving on 17th May 2013.

The Art of Giving is not just about monetary donations; it's about offering one's time, skills, and kindness to others. It's a belief that through acts of generosity—whether through giving or volunteering—we cultivate our spiritual growth and contribute to creating a more compassionate and just world. For Prof. Samanta, this philosophy transcends material possessions. It's about sowing seeds of love, empathy, and kindness, and making these values a part of daily life.

He encourages everyone to practice the Art of Giving by offering compliments, appreciating the good deeds of others, and cultivating noble qualities such as love, faith, and goodwill. He believes that through acts of kindness, we can win hearts, heal wounds, and create a ripple effect of positive change in the world. The practice of the Art of Giving is not just an individual act—it is a global movement aimed at establishing a more equitable society.

Through spiritual meditation, Prof. Samanta suggests we can propagate the essence of "Art of Giving", focusing on kindness, generosity, and spreading love to all. His life serves as a testament to this powerful philosophy, showing us that true fulfillment comes not from what we accumulate, but from what we give.

Impact of His Philosophy and Social Work on Society

Prof. Samanta is not only a distinguished educationist, but also a revered philanthropist, spiritual leader, and social activist. His influence extends far beyond the confines of education, touching all facets of society, including the economy, art, culture, and humanity. Through his life's work, Prof. Samanta has become a beacon of hope and change, creating a lasting impact that continues to resonate across communities.

His philosophy has shaped a transformation not just within educational institutions but in the very fabric of society, where his contributions have inspired socio-economic advancement, cultural preservation, and human development. Prof. Samanta's unwavering commitment to the marginalized and underprivileged has sparked a movement for inclusion, empowerment, and compassion, forging new paths for tribal communities and beyond. His work has been a catalyst for bringing about significant societal change, proving that the power of one individual's vision can uplift entire communities and redefine the course of history.

Birth of the Incredible Educational Institution KISS

The nightmarish impressions of Prof. Achyuta Samanta's childhood, marked by poverty, hunger, and ignorance, fueled his deep compassion and a burning desire to create a world where such suffering no longer existed. As

KIIT, the institution that would soon become a symbol of academic excellence, began to take shape, Prof. Samanta had already begun to envision a dream far greater than his own success. He was determined to uplift the marginalized indigenous tribal children of Odisha, offering them the gift of education as a powerful tool for empowerment.

In 1993, this vision took the form of the Kalinga Institute of Social Sciences (KISS), a humble school offering free education, lodging, and boarding to tribal children. With the firm belief that **"illiteracy breeds poverty and literacy eradicates it,"** Prof. Samanta's initiative began as a small but steadfast school. Over the years, this fledgling institution blossomed into a monumental success, evolving into the world's largest tribal residential school, with over 30,000 students receiving free education from Kindergarten to Post-graduation. The children of the poorest-of-the-poor communities are now provided not only with education but also with modern amenities, state-of-the-art technology, and the promise of a brighter future. KISS stands today as a shining testament to the power of education and compassion, a beacon of hope for indigenous communities across the globe.

Real Transformation of Tribals

Prof. Achyuta Samanta's unwavering vision has always been to provide quality education and holistic development for the poorest indigenous tribal children. His goal is not only to equip them with education but to empower them with skills and vocational training, ensuring they can thrive alongside mainstream society. Under his nurturing guidance, tribal children have blossomed, breaking barriers and achieving what was once thought impossible. These children have represented India on the global sports stage and excelled in competitive examinations, proving Prof. Samanta's firm belief that, given the right opportunities, they can perform at the same level as, or even surpass, their more privileged counterparts.

Over the last decade, KISS has celebrated 100% success rates, with zero dropouts—a remarkable achievement in itself. Beyond academics, the students of KISS have shown an exceptional aptitude in sports, particularly in rugby. Although rugby is not widely popular in Odisha, let alone among its tribal communities, KISS students have embraced the sport with passion and skill, proving that talent knows no boundaries.

Prof. Samanta's legacy is one of transformation—one where even the most disadvantaged have the opportunity to rise, shine, and contribute meaningfully to society. His vision is slowly becoming a reality: an era where every tribal child, irrespective of their background, is given the tools to succeed and where their voice will echo as loudly as those from more affluent communities. In time, the world will surely remember Prof. Samanta not only as a champion of tribal education but as the harbinger of a new, inclusive era.

Changing Impressions of the Highest Possibilities

Under the personal guidance and care of Prof. Achyuta Samanta, the boys of KISS achieved an extraordinary feat that stunned the world—defeating the mighty South African rugby team 19-5 in the finals of the Rugby World Championship in London in 2006. This monumental achievement was not a one-time miracle. Just recently, the team triumphed in six out of eight matches in Australia, further cementing their place as a force to be reckoned with.

To play—and to win—against such formidable opponents on foreign soil is a triumph in itself. Yet, the question remains: how did the impossible become possible? The answer lies in the unwavering determination and vision of Prof. Samanta. Despite being pushed to the brink by poverty, he dared to dream of a world where even the most disadvantaged, those in the lowest strata of society, could stand tall and compete on equal footing.

This was no ordinary dream. It was a vision that defied all odds, and in those moments, Prof. Samanta embodied Napoleon's words: **"Impossible is a word found only in the dictionary of fools."** For him, the dream was always just within reach. And through his relentless grit and belief, the impossible became reality.

Creating a world-class rugby team from among tribal youths, who had never even heard of the sport before, was nothing short of a miracle. Yet, it was a testament to Prof. Samanta's resilience and his unshakable belief in the potential of every individual, regardless of their background. His achievements with KISS and the rugby team are not just about victory on the field—they are a beacon of hope, proving that with vision, determination, and heart, even the most improbable dreams can come true.

Qualitative Change in Tribal Uplift

Prof. Achyuta Samanta dared to bring a revolution into the lives of tribal children by introducing them to the game of rugby—a sport considered alien to them and to the state of Odisha. In a country where sports and sportsmen are often not given the true spirit of encouragement they deserve, Samanta recognized the untapped potential in the eyes of these tribal boys.

In Odisha, where the per capita income is a meagre thousand rupees a year, tribal children often live on wild roots, tubers, leaves, and insects. Their daily existence is a constant struggle for survival, with poverty gripping every aspect of their lives. In such a world, concepts like food, clothing, and education are luxuries far beyond their reach. Yet, Prof. Samanta dared to dream differently for these children—he saw their latent potential not just for survival, but for success, even in fields previously unimaginable to them.

Bringing the tribal children out of poverty was not just about providing basic necessities like food and clothing. It was about offering them the chance to dream, to thrive, and to rise above their circumstances. Samanta's greatest gift to these children was not only the chance to receive education from **Kindergarten to Post-Graduation (KG to PG),** but also to see them achieving excellence, earning recognition on the global stage, and proudly showing the world that they are, indeed, Change Agents.

It takes immense conviction to lift children from such dire poverty and nurture them into champions of change. For Samanta, that conviction was the only currency he needed. His belief that education, combined with care and opportunity, could transform lives has become a testament to the power of dreams and dedication. Today, the tribal children of KISS stand as living proof that with the right guidance, they can conquer any obstacle and make a mark in the world that once seemed beyond their reach.

International Journey and Achievements of the Tribals

Prof. Achyuta Samanta's journey is a testament to one man's indomitable will against all odds. The task of hiring international coaches to train tribal boys, many of whom had never worn shoes, stepped out of their remote forest huts, or even boarded a train, let alone a plane, was nothing short of audacious. Yet, Samanta embraced this challenge with remarkable courage and unwavering passion. His bold experiment has yielded extraordinary results, and today, the world bears witness to the remarkable transformation.

Building an international team from scratch, without any official or financial backing, and with no prior experience in managing professional sports teams, is an achievement that stands unmatched in history. This is not just a personal triumph for Samanta, but a victory for the underprivileged tribal youth, who now stand shoulder to shoulder with global athletes. This is merely the beginning of a long and promising journey ahead.

KISS: Touching Hearts, Drawing Global Attention

The success story of KISS, born from the dream of bridging the socioeconomic gap for tribal children, has not only impacted lives but captured the hearts and minds of the world. Its achievements have attracted the attention and support of major global organizations like UNDP, UNICEF, UNESCO, UNFPA, and even the US Federal Government. These institutions have actively engaged in projects to uplift the tribal students of KISS.

Leaders from all walks of life—Presidents, Prime Ministers, Chief Ministers, Nobel Laureates, diplomats, media magnates, and renowned activists—have visited KISS, each leaving in awe of the transformative impact it has created. These distinguished visitors were astonished by the scale and uniqueness of this endeavor, which stands as one of the greatest feats of social transformation in modern history.

KISS is not merely an educational institution; it is a living testament to the possibility of change. It is steadily marching forward, contributing significantly towards achieving the United Nations Millennium Development Goals, proving that even the most marginalized can rise to greatness when given the opportunity to succeed. KISS is an enduring symbol of hope, dedication, and the power of education to change lives, and it continues to inspire the world.

Recognizing Service to Humanity Globally

The journey towards a world free from hunger, suffering, conflict, and bloodshed begins with a single step, often taken quietly, without fanfare or recognition. The outcomes are seldom immediate, and the most significant victories often go unnoticed. The path is long and at times fraught with pain, but every step taken in the pursuit of this noble goal adds depth and purpose to the venture. For Prof. Samanta, this path is one of compassion, a deep-rooted belief in the power of the human heart to change the world.

A compassionate heart, unbound by borders or sectarian divides, is universal in its reach. It transcends regional, cultural, and religious boundaries, seeking only to alleviate suffering wherever it is found. To celebrate such hearts and the extraordinary service to humanity they embody, Prof. Samanta instituted the prestigious **KISS HUMANITARIAN AWARD**. This annual award honors individuals whose dedication to humanitarian causes has made a profound and lasting impact on the world.

Among the distinguished recipients of this honor are some of the most prominent figures from across the globe, whose contributions have echoed far and wide:

- **Ms. Edna Bomo Molewa**, Noted Social Worker and Minister in the South African National Assembly
- Prof. Ham Kee-Sun, President and Founder of Hanseo University, South Korea
- **Sir Anerood Jugnauth**, His Excellency, the President of Mauritius
- **Rt. Hon Lord Nicholas Addison Phillips**, President (Chief Justice) of the Supreme Court of the United Kingdom

- **His Excellency Lyonchhen Jigmi Y. Thinley,** Hon'ble Prime Minister of the Royal Government of Bhutan
- Honourable **Ratan Tata** – The eminent industrialist and philanthropist was honored with the **KISS Humanitarian Award** for his unwavering commitment to social welfare and inclusive development, uplifting millions across India.

Honourable **Bill Gates** – Renowned for his global philanthropic initiatives through the **Bill & Melinda Gates Foundation**, he received the award for his outstanding contributions to healthcare, education, and poverty alleviation worldwide.

- Honourable **Dalai Lama** – The spiritual leader was recognized for his lifelong dedication to **peace, compassion, and education**, inspiring humanitarian efforts across the world.

These extraordinary individuals, recognized for their unwavering commitment to service, exemplify the profound impact that compassionate leadership can have on the global stage. The KISS HUMANITARIAN AWARD not only celebrates their work but also serves as a reminder that true service to humanity knows no borders. It is an enduring tribute to those who dedicate their lives to making the world a better place, just as Prof. Samanta has done with his vision for the future.

Service for Mother and Motherland

The establishment of KISS is just one expression of Prof. Samanta's multifaceted character, yet it encapsulates his deep-rooted values—respect for his mother's wishes and a lifelong commitment to his origins. Prof. Samanta's devotion to his roots can be seen in how he transformed his humble, remote village of Kalarabanka into a thriving model of progress. Once a village entrenched in poverty, Kalarabanka now shines as a beacon of development, offering the same conveniences as any urban area.

Through his tireless efforts, Prof. Samanta has given the village a divine touch of his vision and love, turning it into a *Model Village* and eventually a *Model Panchayat*. The growth of Kalarabanka has sparked similar transformations across neighboring villages, catalyzing a ripple effect of development throughout the Kalarabanka Panchayat. The village has become an educational hub, offering both vernacular and English-medium schools, ensuring that quality education is within reach

for every child. It proudly holds the distinction of being the first village in India to provide 100% health insurance coverage for its citizens—a groundbreaking achievement.

Beyond these milestones, Kalarabanka has embraced all the modern amenities that enhance the quality of life—clean drinking water systems, a 50-bedded hospital, postal and banking services, telephone and internet connectivity, temples, and community halls. But perhaps most beautifully, under Prof. Samanta's guidance, the village has nurtured its cultural heritage, with annual community festivals that celebrate local traditions and bring together the spirit of unity.

This transformation is a powerful tribute to the land that raised him—a profound act of giving back to the mother and the motherland that shaped his childhood. It is a living testament to his unwavering belief that true service begins at home, with love and dedication toward one's roots. Kalarabanka, now flourishing with life and opportunity, stands as a reflection of Prof. Samanta's gratitude, vision, and deep sense of responsibility toward both his mother and his homeland.

Strengthening Art and Culture

Prof. Samanta's vision goes beyond the confines of education and social work; it extends deeply into the preservation and promotion of Odisha's rich cultural heritage. True to his philosophy of honoring mother, motherland, and mother tongue, Prof. Samanta has worked tirelessly to safeguard and enrich the literature, art, and culture of Odisha. His passion for the arts and his commitment to his roots led to the founding of Kadambini Media Pvt. Ltd. in 2000. Through this platform, he introduced two groundbreaking publications: *The* **"Kadambini"**,  Odisha's first-ever family feature magazine, and *The* **"Kunikatha"**, the first magazine dedicated to children in Odia.

These magazines quickly gained prominence, not just because of their content, but also due to the impeccable taste and artistic touch that Prof. Samanta infused into them, setting new standards in the region. Both publications have since become household names, and their continued success is a reflection of his vision to promote Odia culture in a contemporary context.

Understanding the power of modern media, Prof. Samanta also recognized films as a powerful tool for social change and raising awareness. His company produced *"Kathantara"*, an award-winning feature film in Odia that poignantly portrayed the aftermath of the devastating super-cyclone, shedding light on the struggles of those affected. Through such initiatives, Prof. Samanta has displayed an unwavering commitment to using various forms of art to serve humanity and address social issues, blending his love for culture with his deep-seated drive for positive change.

His contributions to the arts reflect the versatility that defines his character, driven by an innate desire to serve society and honor the culture that shaped him. Prof. Samanta's efforts continue to inspire, ensuring that the cultural tapestry of Odisha remains vibrant, accessible, and relevant to generations to come.

Strengthening the Local Economy

Prof. A. Samanta's remarkable vision has reshaped not just educational paradigms but also the very fabric of the local economy. Recognized among the top 15 social entrepreneurs in the world by the Edge Foundation, USA, Prof. Samanta has applied his entrepreneurial genius to tackle some of society's most pressing challenges. His profound ability to identify systemic flaws and develop innovative solutions has created lasting impact.

One of the most striking examples of his transformative approach is the establishment of KIIT University. The area that was once infamous for criminal activities and rampant unemployment has undergone a complete metamorphosis. What was once a neglected region is now a thriving hub of commerce, education, and industry. Today, the locality hosts a variety of industries, technical and professional institutions, shopping complexes, banks, and financial establishments, all of which contribute to direct and indirect employment opportunities for the local population.

This economic revolution is a testament to Prof. Samanta's unique blend of innovation, motivation, and critical thinking. His relentless drive to solve complex social problems through education and enterprise has not only elevated the area's economic standing but has also set a model for how social entrepreneurship can uplift entire communities. Prof. Samanta's work proves that when vision, dedication, and action come together, even the most challenged communities can witness a dramatic transformation.

Preaching Simple Living and High Thinking

Prof. Samanta's life is a living tribute to the Gandhian ideals of simplicity, humility, and selfless service. Despite his global success, his personal life remains grounded in the most basic of values. Today, he could easily afford the luxuries of life, but to him, these hold little value. His life speaks volumes through its simplicity—his modest, vegetarian meals, his unpretentious attire, and the warm, inviting smile that reflects the kindness in his heart.

He has never craved power or the comforts of wealth. Rather, he finds his greatest fulfillment in giving—whether it's his time, his compassion, or his resources. To him, the true luxury lies in serving others. This profound sense of simplicity and sacrifice has been the cornerstone of his success, driving the rapid growth of the two monumental institutions he founded and others he has touched. His personal struggle, his willingness to live with the bare minimum, and his deep devotion to humanity have earned him respect far beyond material accomplishments.

Prof. Samanta's life has inspired admiration from every corner of the globe. Renowned regional, national, and international publications like *Time Magazine, Outlook, India Today,* **and** *Reader's Digest* have recognized his work and vision. Esteemed universities and governments across the world have honored him with doctorates and other prestigious awards. Yet, his greatest recognition comes from the countless lives he has touched, driven by his unwavering belief in simplicity, high thinking, and the relentless pursuit of a better world for all.

Promoting Service to Mankind is Service to God

Prof. Achyuta Samanta, a man of a thousand dreams, chases each one with unwavering determination, transforming them from mere visions into tangible realities. For many, dreams often remain elusive, nothing more than illusions or mirages. But for Samanta, the pursuit of a noble cause is fueled by faith, steadfast effort, and careful maneuvering—ingredients that inevitably lead to success. This has been his guiding mantra, one that has shaped his remarkable journey.

Losing his father at the age of four and growing up in poverty, Samanta could have easily succumbed to life's harsh realities. With no stable income and multiple mouths to feed, most would have been overwhelmed by despair. But Samanta's indomitable spirit refused to yield. From his humble beginnings, walking from nursery classes to a Master's degree in Chemistry,

Samanta left an unforgettable impression on everyone he encountered. Teachers remember him as a brilliant student, the elders of his village recall him as a helping hand, and the local priest remembers him as a devout devotee, bringing flowers and Tulsi for the deities.

The blessings he gathered along the way were not just acts of kindness, but investments in his future—investments that ultimately culminated in the creation of two monumental institutions, KISS and KIIT. These institutions not only brought him personal glory, but also pride to the land that nurtured him, the state whose air he breathed, whose water he drank, and whose spiritual ethos inspired him to dream.

Prof. Samanta has truly blazed a trail of service to humanity, proving that service to mankind is indeed the highest form of service to God. His life is a testament to the transformative power of faith, perseverance, and a deep commitment to the welfare of others.

Philosophy of education

Prof. Achyuta Samanta's educational philosophy is a harmonious blend of Idealism, Pragmatism, and Naturalism, seamlessly integrating these diverse strands into a unified approach. He views education not just as a means of academic development, but as a **potent tool for empowerment and societal transformation.** Through the world-renowned Kalinga Institute of Social Sciences (KISS), Prof. Samanta has given practical expression to his educational ideals, creating an institution that embodies the transformative power of education.

His philosophy reflects a vision deeply influenced by the principles of the industrial revolution—focused on the empowerment of tribal communities, their mainstreaming into society, and introducing them to the modern world, all while eradicating outdated dogmas. Above all, his focus is on **Holistic Education**, a concept that strives for the all-around development of individuals, addressing not only knowledge acquisition but also the development of life skills that empower people to thrive in society.

Prof. Samanta firmly believes that education has two vital purposes: the **first** is the development of knowledge, and the **second** is providing the skills necessary for meaningful employment, enabling individuals to lead successful lives. This dual approach forms the foundation of his educational beliefs. He holds two fundamental principles at the core of his philosophy:

1. **Changeability of Ideas**: No idea or educational principle is everlasting or universally applicable. Education, curricula, and objectives must evolve according to the changing needs of society. The dynamism of society demands an educational process that is flexible, responsive, and adaptive to new challenges.

Example: Dynamic Curriculum and Skill Integration at KISS

In alignment with Prof. Achyuta Samanta's philosophy that no educational idea or principle is permanent, KISS continuously revises its curriculum to meet the evolving needs of society. A striking example is the institution's recent integration of digital literacy, coding, and AI awareness into the school curriculum — a move that reflects responsiveness to the growing significance of technology in every sector.

Additionally, KISS has expanded its focus beyond traditional classroom teaching to include life skills education, financial literacy, entrepreneurship, environmental sustainability, and global citizenship education. These updates ensure that tribal students are not only academically prepared but are also equipped with contemporary competencies to thrive in modern society.

Teaching methods at KISS have also evolved — shifting from lecture-based delivery to experiential learning, activity-based pedagogy, and the use of smart classrooms, enabling students to connect education with real-world challenges. These adaptive steps demonstrate how KISS embodies the idea that education must remain flexible, relevant, and socially responsive.

2. **Utility and Human Welfare**: Education's true value lies in its capacity to serve humanity. It should always be practical and useful, directly contributing to human welfare. For Prof. Samanta, an education that does not contribute to the betterment of human lives, particularly the most marginalized, is incomplete. Therefore, educational practices must be continually refined to maximize their benefit for human society.

Example: Free Holistic Education for Marginalized Tribal Children

Prof. Achyuta Samanta's unwavering commitment to human welfare is best exemplified through KISS's mission to provide completely free education, food, clothing, accommodation, and healthcare to over 30,000 tribal children — many of whom come from extremely impoverished and underserved communities.

This model ensures that education at KISS is not just academic but life-sustaining. It empowers students with practical knowledge, vocational training, life skills, and access to dignified living conditions — all of which contribute directly to the upliftment of entire tribal communities.

KISS transforms education into a tool of social justice, making it both useful and deeply relevant to human welfare, especially for those who need it most. It is a living example of how education, when rooted in compassion and utility, becomes a powerful force for inclusive development.

For Prof. Samanta, **Holistic Education** is not a mere academic pursuit—it is a living philosophy that adapts to the times and seeks to meet the varied needs of society. It is this very philosophy that guides the creation of opportunities for the tribal communities, helping them overcome centuries of disadvantage and paving the way for a future of greater equality and prosperity. Education, in his view, must remain flexible, dynamic, and grounded in the principles of social justice, continuously evolving to meet the needs of an ever-changing world.

Key Pillars of Prof. Achyuta Samanta's Educational Philosophy

Prof. Achyuta Samanta, the visionary founder of Kalinga Institute of Social Sciences (KISS) and Kalinga Institute of Industrial Technology (KIIT), has articulated a transformative educational philosophy grounded in equity, compassion, and empowerment. The following four pillars encapsulate his holistic approach:

Key pillars(four) of his educational philosophy include:

1. **Holistic Development through 3Rs, 3Hs, and 3Es:**
   Prof. Achyuta Samanta advocates for an integrated and balanced approach to education that moves beyond traditional academics to promote holistic development. His educational philosophy incorporates the 3Rs—Reading, Writing, and Arithmetic—as foundational literacies, along with the 3Hs—Head (cognitive development), Hand (practical and vocational skills), and Heart (emotional and moral values)—to cultivate well-rounded learners. Furthermore, his inclusion of the 3Es—Educate, Empower, and Enable—ensures that education serves as a transformative force that builds knowledge, confidence, and competence in every learner.

   This triadic framework nurtures individuals who are intellectually sharp, emotionally resilient, socially responsible, and practically skilled. By aligning academic rigor with humanistic and life-oriented values, Prof. Samanta's model prepares students not only for personal success but also for meaningful contributions to society, especially in the context of nation-building and inclusive growth.

2. **Value-Based Learning as a Foundation:**
   Prof. Achyuta Samanta strongly believes that true education must be rooted in core human values. Drawing inspiration from his philosophy of the "Art of Giving", he emphasizes the integration of gratitude, empathy, compassion, honesty, and integrity into both pedagogy and institutional culture. These values are not peripheral but central to character building and civic responsibility. By embedding ethical principles into education, Prof. Samanta aims to nurture socially conscious, morally grounded, and emotionally mature individuals who contribute meaningfully to a just, peaceful, and sustainable society.

3. **Inclusive and Equitable Education for All:**
   A cornerstone of Prof. Samanta's mission is the democratization of education—ensuring that every child, regardless of caste, class, gender, ability, or geography, has access to quality learning. His work through the Kalinga Institute of Social Sciences (KISS)—which provides free education, food, healthcare, and accommodation to over 30,000 tribal children—is a global model of inclusive and equitable education. By bridging social and economic divides, Prof. Samanta demonstrates how compassion-driven leadership can dismantle systemic barriers and foster true educational justice and social integration.

4. **Education as a Tool for Empowerment and Transformation:**
   For Prof. Samanta, education is a transformational force that extends far beyond classrooms. It is a catalyst for social upliftment, capable of breaking the cycle of poverty, dismantling inequality, and empowering individuals to shape their destinies. Through his institutions, he has created ecosystems where learners—especially from marginalized backgrounds—gain not only academic knowledge but also life skills, confidence, and agency. His model shows how education can lead to personal dignity, community development, and the emergence of socially responsible leaders equipped to transform their communities and the nation at large.

Table: Four Pillars of Prof. Achyuta Samanta's Educational Philosophy

Pillar	Description	Key Focus Areas
1. Holistic Development	Education should integrate the **3Rs** (Reading, Writing, Arithmetic), **3Hs** (Head – cognitive, Hand – practical, Heart – emotional), and **3Es** (Educate, Empower, Enable) to promote comprehensive growth.	Intellectual Growth, Practical Skills, Emotional Intelligence, Empowerment
2. Value-Based Learning	Rooted in the philosophy of the **"Art of Giving"**, it emphasizes cultivating core human values like *gratitude, empathy, honesty,* and *integrity* to nurture ethically grounded individuals.	Character Formation, Ethical Citizenship, Social Responsibility
3. Inclusion and Equity	Focuses on **universal access** to quality education, particularly for **marginalized, tribal, and underprivileged communities**, ensuring that no child is left behind.	Educational Equity, Social Justice, Inclusive Growth
4. Education for Empowerment	Envisions education as a **transformative tool** to break the cycle of poverty, uplift entire communities, and develop self-reliant, socially conscious individuals.	Personal Upliftment, Community Development, Self-Reliance

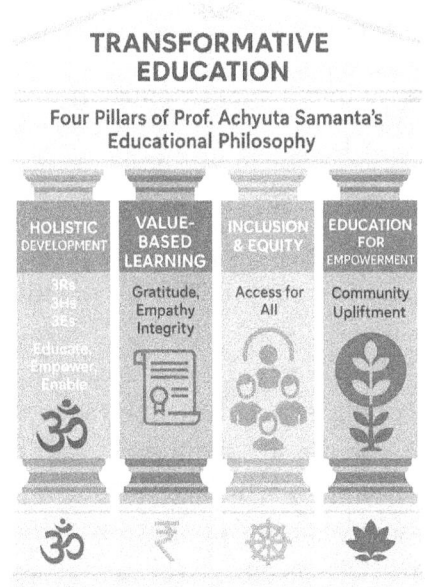

Meaning of Education

Prof. Achyuta Samanta envisions education as a process of drawing out the innate potential of every child and nurturing it through a supportive and inclusive learning environment. He believes that education should provide all necessary opportunities to enable children to flourish as complete human beings.

According to Prof. Achyuta Samanta, education must emphasize a balanced and holistic approach that nurtures the **3Rs** (Reading, Writing, Arithmetic) for foundational literacy, the **3Hs** (Head, Hand, Heart) representing cognitive, practical, and emotional development, and the **3Es** (Educate, Empower, Enable) which signify the transformative power of education. This comprehensive model promotes not only **intellectual and academic excellence,** but also **emotional intelligence, ethical grounding,** and **practical life skills**. Prof. Samanta advocates for an education system that cultivates **well-rounded individuals**—capable, compassionate, and socially responsible—prepared to contribute meaningfully to their communities and to the nation.

His vision advocates creating an ecosystem within schools that ensures every child is equipped with the resources, care, and guidance needed to achieve their full potential. This approach fosters not just academic excellence but also life skills, compassion, and resilience. Education, as envisioned by Prof. Samanta, is not merely about imparting knowledge but also about preparing students to lead meaningful, ethical, and fulfilling lives.

By emphasizing these aspects, Prof. Samanta aligns education with the broader goal of shaping students into responsible and compassionate global citizens.

Prof. Samanta believes on the following explanation of his Philosophy

1. **Holistic Development**
   - The focus on the **3Rs** (*Reading, Writing, Arithmetic*) ensures a strong academic foundation, equipping learners with essential literacy and numeracy skills.
   - The inclusion of the **3Hs** (*Head, Hand, Heart*) emphasizes the balanced development of **intellectual abilities** (Head), **practical and vocational competencies** (Hand), and **emotional and moral values** (Heart), fostering well-rounded growth.
   - Additionally, the integration of the **3Es** (*Educate, Empower, Enable*) reflects Prof. Samanta's vision of education as a **transformative force**—

one that not only imparts knowledge but also **empowers learners with confidence and skills**, and **enables them to contribute meaningfully to society**.
- Together, the 3Rs, 3Hs, and 3Es form a **comprehensive educational framework** that promotes **academic excellence, life skills, emotional resilience**, and **social responsibility**.

2. Opportunities for Flourishing
- Prof. Achyuta Samanta's educational philosophy places strong emphasis on creating **nurturing, inclusive, and resource-rich learning environments**, especially for students from **marginalized and underserved communities**. His vision ensures that **no child is deprived of opportunities** due to socio-economic disadvantages. Schools must not only provide access to quality education, but also offer **emotional support, nutritious food, healthcare, and mentorship**—enabling every learner to flourish in all dimensions of life.

3. Humanistic Approach
- Beyond academic performance, Prof. Samanta advocates for a **deeply humanistic approach** to education. Institutions must instill **compassion, empathy, respect, and a sense of collective responsibility** in their students. Education, in this view, becomes a means of **moral awakening and social transformation**, producing individuals who are not only **knowledgeable** but also **ethically committed to the well-being of others**, especially the less privileged.

4. Practical Implication
- Institutions like **KISS (Kalinga Institute of Social Sciences)** and **KIIT** serve as **living embodiments** of Prof. Samanta's philosophy. These institutions go beyond classroom teaching to offer **holistic education**— combining academic instruction with life skills, vocational training, emotional development, and cultural grounding.

For example, a KISSan is not just expected to excel in academics but also to **demonstrate gratitude, empathy, and community responsibility** in real life. A practical manifestation of this can be seen when **KISS graduates return to their communities as teachers, health workers, or social leaders**, using their education not just for personal success but to **uplift others**—thereby **comprehending and living** the philosophy they were nurtured in.

Definition of Education

The concept of *education* is multifaceted, encompassing intellectual, emotional, social, and ethical dimensions. It is a process that nurtures the whole individual—mind, body, and spirit—while equipping them with the skills and values needed to contribute meaningfully to society. Over time, the definition of education has evolved, shaped by societal needs, cultural contexts, and individual aspirations.

Prof. Achyuta Samanta, a visionary proponent of holistic education, offers profound insights into the transformative power of education. His philosophy reflects a commitment to fostering well-rounded individuals who are not only knowledgeable but also compassionate, resilient, and socially responsible. His definitions emphasize education as a means to empower, uplift, and create opportunities, particularly for the marginalized and underprivileged.

Prof. Samanta's Perspectives on Education

1. **"Education is the only weapon to slay any evil."**
   - Prof. Samanta views education as the ultimate tool to address societal challenges, eradicate inequalities, and foster a just and equitable world. Holistic education, in this sense, integrates ethical values, critical thinking, and problem-solving skills to combat societal evils.
2. **"Giving education to a deprived child is like giving sight to the blind."**
   - This analogy underscores the life-changing power of education. Holistic education, as envisioned by Prof. Samanta, goes beyond academics to nurture the emotional and social well-being of children, enabling them to envision a brighter future.
3. **"Poverty breeds illiteracy, and literacy drives away poverty."**
   - Prof. Samanta emphasizes the symbiotic relationship between education and poverty alleviation. By addressing not just intellectual needs but also emotional, social, and ethical aspects, holistic education helps break the cycle of poverty and fosters self-reliance and dignity.
4. **"Half education is more harmful than no education."**
   - Partial or incomplete education can lead to limited understanding, narrow perspectives, and misinformed decision-making, ultimately hindering personal and societal growth. In contrast,

holistic education—as envisioned by Prof. Achyuta Samanta—emphasizes the integration of the 3Rs (Reading, Writing, Arithmetic), the 3Hs (Head for intellectual development, Hand for practical skills, Heart for emotional and moral values), and the 3Es (Educate, Empower, Enable).This comprehensive framework prepares individuals to navigate the complexities of life with clarity, competence, compassion, and a strong sense of social responsibility, ensuring that education becomes a force for empowerment and transformation, not just information.

5. **"Given opportunity, the weak too can excel."**
   - Rooted in the ethos of KISS, this perspective celebrates the transformative potential of inclusive and equitable education. Prof. Samanta's holistic approach recognizes the importance of creating an environment where every individual's intellectual, emotional, and social potentials are nurtured.

A Holistic Vision of Education

Prof. Samanta's philosophy integrates the principles of **holistic education**, which seeks to nurture the whole child by addressing their cognitive, emotional, physical, and spiritual growth. This vision ensures that education is not just about academic success but also about cultivating compassion, resilience, and social responsibility.

His understanding of education is dynamic, adapting to the needs of changing times while staying true to the goal of human flourishing. His work at KISS and KIIT exemplifies this holistic approach, providing students with comprehensive resources, fostering creativity, and instilling core values to prepare them for life's challenges.

Education as Transformation

For Prof. Samanta, education is a transformative force that bridges societal gaps, uplifts communities, and fosters individual well-being. Holistic education, in his view, empowers learners to develop not just knowledge but also the character, empathy, and skills necessary to thrive in an interconnected world. His philosophy encourages educators and institutions to view education as a lifelong process of self-discovery and community building.

Prof. Samanta's philosophy acknowledges that the meaning and function of education must adapt to changing contexts. His interpretations are not confined to a single definition but are drawn from his lived experiences, interactions with educators, students, and global leaders, and his unwavering commitment to inclusivity and empowerment.

For Prof. Samanta, education is far more than the acquisition of knowledge; it is a transformative force that nurtures individuals, uplifts communities, and builds a more equitable world. His sayings resonate with his mission of providing quality education to those who need it most, making his work a living testament to the true essence of education.

His Mission of Life Through Education

In the 21st century, many visionary educational entrepreneurs emphasize that the mission of education should enable students to acquire skills and knowledge that empower them to secure employment or practice a profession, thereby becoming self-reliant. Globally, education in many contexts has become an assembly line where it is often reduced to the process of "matriculate, inculcate, and graduate."

However, Prof. Achyuta Samanta's mission of life through education transcends this narrow utilitarian view. While his institutions like KIIT and KISS boast state-of-the-art infrastructure, modern amenities, and advanced technological facilities, his primary goal is not merely to prepare students for jobs. Instead, he envisions education as a tool to nurture good human beings who are grounded in values, ethics, and compassion.

One of his notable sayings encapsulates this mission: **"Krutangya Hua, Krutaghna Hua Nahin"** (Be grateful, not ungrateful). He often shares this profound thought with his students and the larger society, emphasizing gratitude as a fundamental human value. Prof. Samanta views education as a means to serve the ultimate purpose of life: uplifting individuals and communities through values-based, skill-oriented, and spiritually enriched learning.

Key Components of His Mission Through Education

Prof. Samanta's mission focuses on addressing societal challenges and fostering holistic development through education. His educational initiatives aim to:

1. **Eradicate Poverty and Hunger Through Education**
   Prof. Samanta believes that education is the most powerful tool to break the cycle of poverty and hunger, especially for tribal and underprivileged communities. Through institutions like the Kalinga Institute of Social Sciences (KISS), thousands of children

from remote and marginalized areas receive free, holistic education that includes academic learning, nutritious meals, healthcare, and residential facilities.

Example: A child from a tribal village, once engaged in daily wage labor to support their family, is enrolled at KISS. With access to structured education, balanced nutrition, and a safe environment, the child transitions from survival-based existence to academic excellence. Over time, they gain confidence, complete higher studies, and secure meaningful employment. This holistic educational support not only uplifts the individual but also contributes to breaking intergenerational poverty and uplifting the entire family and community.

2. **Empower Through Education**

   By offering inclusive, quality education, he aims to empower students with the knowledge, skills, and confidence needed to lead independent and meaningful lives.

   Example: For instance, a student from a remote tribal area, who had never stepped into a classroom before, gains access to structured learning at KISS. Through digital literacy, vocational training, and life-skills education, the student becomes self-reliant, secures a job in the service sector, and supports their family financially—demonstrating the empowering force of education.

3. **Transform 'Liability' into 'Asset' Through Education**

   Prof. Samanta's vision is to turn perceived societal "liabilities," such as marginalized and tribal children, into invaluable assets by nurturing their potential and abilities.

   Example: In the KISS model, tribal children, once considered a societal burden due to their socio-economic conditions, are provided with free education, healthcare, and life skills training. As a result, these children, who were once dependent on charity, grow into educated individuals who contribute back to their communities—becoming teachers, doctors, and community leaders—transforming the perception of liability into an asset.

4. **Bring Tribal Children to the Mainstream**

   His mission includes bridging the gap between tribal children and the rest of society, enabling them to compete on equal footing while preserving their unique heritage and culture.

   Example: At KISS, tribal children are not only taught traditional academics but also learn digital literacy, science, and mathematics, helping them compete in mainstream education and the job market.

Simultaneously, they participate in cultural programs that celebrate their heritage, ensuring that their identity is preserved while they engage with the broader society.

5. **Enable Students to Lead Decent Lives in the 21st Century**

   Education, according to Prof. Samanta, must equip students to avail themselves of modern opportunities, lead dignified lives, and contribute to society's progress.

   Example: A student from a tribal community, after completing their education at KISS, gains skills in both vocational training and modern technology. They use these skills to secure a job in the urban job market, achieve financial independence, and live a dignified life, contributing to society's development through their work in sectors like healthcare, education, and technology.

6. **Preserve Tribal Heritage and Culture**

   Prof. Samanta emphasizes the importance of preserving the rich heritage, traditions, and values of tribal communities, ensuring they are celebrated rather than lost in modernization.

   Example: At KISS, tribal children learn not only modern subjects but also traditional dance, music, and crafts. This dual approach ensures that while they gain modern education, their cultural identity remains intact. Annual cultural festivals held at KISS showcase tribal art and traditions, allowing students to celebrate their heritage proudly and share it with the larger society.

7. **Nurture Tribal Children as 'Change Agents'**

   He believes that educating tribal children will empower them to uplift their communities, serving as role models and leaders for positive change.

   Example: After completing their education, many KISS alumni return to their villages as health workers, teachers, and community leaders, actively contributing to the development of their communities. They are seen as role models, showing younger generations that education can lead to transformative change and inspire others to follow their path.

8. **Enhance Quality of Life Across Generations**

   By providing education, Prof. Samanta envisions a better quality of life for tribal children and their future generations, alleviating them from the hardships faced by their forefathers

Example: A student from a tribal community who graduates from KISS goes on to secure employment, contributing financially to their family. Over time, this family's socio-economic status improves, ensuring that future generations of children in the family will have access to quality education, breaking the cycle of poverty and improving their quality of life for years to come.

Alignment with Millennium Development Goals (MDGs)

Prof. Samanta's mission aligns seamlessly with the **Millennium Development Goals** set by the United Nations. Through his initiatives, he addresses these global objectives within his educational framework:

1. **Eradicate Extreme Poverty and Hunger**
   - His institutions provide free education, accommodation, healthcare, and nutrition, ensuring the holistic well-being of students from impoverished backgrounds.
2. **Achieve Universal Primary Education**
   - By offering accessible and quality education to marginalized groups, Prof. Samanta works toward universal primary and secondary education, particularly for tribal children.
3. **Promote Gender Equality and Empower Women**
   - A significant proportion of students at KISS are girls, reflecting his commitment to empowering women through education and promoting gender equity.
4. **Reduce Child Mortality**
   - By addressing the basic health and nutritional needs of tribal children, his institutions indirectly contribute to reducing child mortality rates in tribal communities.
5. **Improve Maternal Health**
   - His educational outreach includes community programs that promote awareness about maternal health, benefiting the families of tribal students.
6. **Combat HIV/AIDS, Malaria, and Other Diseases**
   - KISS provides health education and preventive healthcare to students, ensuring they grow up healthy and aware of critical health issues.
7. **Ensure Environmental Sustainability**
   - Through curriculum and campus practices, such as eco-

friendly infrastructure and environmental education, his institutions emphasize sustainable living.

8. **Develop a Global Partnership for Development**
    - Prof. Samanta's work has garnered international recognition, fostering partnerships with global organizations to promote education and social development.

Prof. Achyuta Samanta's mission of life through education is a beacon of hope for those left behind by traditional systems. By aligning his vision with the MDGs, he has created a transformative model of education that not only uplifts individuals but also strengthens communities and addresses global challenges. His work exemplifies how education can serve as a holistic tool to shape better individuals and a better world.

Alignment with Sustainable Development Goals (SDGs)

Prof. Samanta's educational initiatives align with the **17 Sustainable Development Goals (SDGs)** outlined by the United Nations, reflecting his commitment to fostering a more equitable, sustainable, and inclusive world. Below is an explanation of how his work addresses each goal:

1. Goal 1: No Poverty

By offering **completely free and comprehensive education**—including not just academic instruction but also **nutrition, healthcare, clothing, and secure accommodation**—to thousands of tribal and underprivileged children, Prof. Samanta's institutions are **breaking the intergenerational cycle of poverty**. His model not only lifts individual families out of poverty but also **creates pathways for sustainable community development**, empowering educated youth to become economically self-reliant and to support their families and local economies. This holistic intervention addresses poverty at both **systemic and grassroots levels**, making education a tool for long-term socio-economic transformation.

2. Goal 2: Zero Hunger

Prof. Samanta's institutions ensure that **every student receives daily nutritious meals**, promoting not only their physical health but also their **cognitive development** and **academic performance**. The provision of these meals is a cornerstone of his educational model, tackling hunger directly while creating an environment where children can focus on learning rather than worrying about food security. By **addressing malnutrition**, his initiatives contribute to the long-term **health and productivity of future generations**, while fostering **a culture of health and well-being** in underserved communities.

3. Goal 3: Good Health and Well-Being

Prof. Samanta's institutions provide **comprehensive healthcare services**, including **regular health check-ups, vaccinations, health education**, and **mental health support**. This holistic approach ensures that students and their families have access to **preventive healthcare**, reducing disease burden and promoting overall well-being. By addressing both physical and mental health needs, Prof. Samanta's initiatives ensure that students are not only **healthy and happy** but also able to fully engage in their education and contribute to the development of their communities. These services also extend to **health awareness programs**, empowering individuals to make informed decisions about their health.

4. Goal 4: Quality Education

Prof. Samanta is committed to providing **inclusive, equitable, and high-quality education** that equips students with the knowledge, skills, and confidence necessary to succeed in the modern world. His institutions, especially **KISS**, emphasize **holistic education** that fosters not only academic excellence but also practical and emotional development. KISS provides a range of **learning resources** including **well-equipped classrooms, digital libraries**, and **vocational training centers**, all designed to support diverse learning needs and ensure **lifelong learning opportunities**. By making **quality education accessible to thousands of tribal children**, Prof. Samanta is fostering a generation capable of tackling future challenges, thus contributing to the **global commitment to education for all**.

5. Goal 5: Gender Equality

Gender equity is a cornerstone of Prof. Samanta's educational philosophy. His initiatives ensure significant representation of **girls** in his institutions, with a particular focus on **empowering them** through education and leadership development. At **KISS, girl students** receive equal access to educational resources, scholarships, and extracurricular activities. The institution actively works to address the gender gap by providing **safe learning environments**, offering **mentorship programs**, and emphasizing **gender-sensitive pedagogy**. Moreover, **KISS organizes initiatives** that challenge societal stereotypes and promote **leadership opportunities** for women, ensuring that tribal girls have the confidence and skills to break barriers and assume leadership roles in their communities. This commitment to **gender equality** helps to cultivate a generation of empowered women who can contribute meaningfully to social and economic development.

6. Goal 6: Clean Water and Sanitation

At **KISS**, ensuring access to **clean drinking water** and **sanitation facilities** is a priority. Both institutions are committed to providing **safe and hygienic** environments for students, with strategically placed water filtration systems, **sanitation facilities**, and **health awareness programs** that encourage proper hygiene practices. These efforts ensure that students have access to **clean water** and **adequate sanitation**, significantly reducing the risks of waterborne diseases and promoting a **healthy campus environment**. The commitment to providing **clean water** is crucial for the physical well-being of students and contributes to their ability to focus on education without the concerns of inadequate health resources.

7. Goal 7: Affordable and Clean Energy

Prof. Samanta's institution, **KISS**, isthe leader in incorporating **renewable energy practices**, with a strong emphasis on **solar power** as a sustainable energy source. The campuses utilize **solar panels**, reducing reliance on non-renewable energy and decreasing their carbon footprint. This commitment to **clean energy** not only ensures that the institutions operate in an environmentally responsible way but also serves as an educational model for students on the importance of **sustainability and climate action**. By integrating **solar energy**, these institutions contribute to global efforts to **combat climate change** while providing affordable and reliable energy solutions for their campuses.

8. Goal 8: Decent Work and Economic Growth

At **KISS**, **skill development programs** and **vocational training** are integral to preparing students for sustainable employment opportunities. The institution offers **hands-on training** in various trades such as **agriculture**, **handicrafts**, **healthcare**, and **technology**, equipping students with the practical skills necessary for both **employment** and **entrepreneurship**. By fostering an environment focused on **self-reliance** and **economic empowerment**, **KISS** helps students secure **stable jobs** or launch their own **businesses**, contributing to **local economic growth**.

9. Goal 9: Industry, Innovation, and Infrastructure

KISS fosters **innovation** through its strong focus on **modern infrastructure** and **technological resources**. The institution is equipped with specialized **vocational training centers** and **innovation hubs** that promote practical learning and **research initiatives**. Through its **training programs** and **workshops**, **KISS** encourages students to think critically, develop innovative solutions, and build **self-sustaining projects** that benefit their communities. These efforts enhance **local industries** and prepare students to meet the evolving demands of the workforce.

10. Goal 10: Reduced Inequalities

KISS directly addresses social inequality by providing **marginalized tribal children** with equal access to **quality education, healthcare, food, and housing**. By offering **free education**, **KISS** breaks down systemic barriers to learning and helps tribal students overcome **historical disadvantages**. This holistic approach allows students to thrive in both **academic and personal growth**, promoting **social inclusion** and enabling them to fully participate in society, irrespective of their background.

11. Goal 11: Sustainable Cities and Communities

At **KISS**, **sustainable development** is a key focus, both within the institution and in its outreach efforts. The institution actively promotes **sustainable agricultural practices** and **environmental education** for tribal communities. By integrating **eco-friendly practices** into daily life and **community projects**, students are empowered to become **ambassadors of sustainability**. Additionally, **KISS** encourages **green infrastructure** and **renewable energy** projects, aiming to create a lasting impact on the **environment** while promoting **social equity** and **community development**.

12. Goal 12: Responsible Consumption and Production

KISS actively promotes **environmental awareness** among students and faculty, encouraging the **responsible use of resources**. Through its campus sustainability initiatives, such as **waste segregation, water conservation**, and the use of **eco-friendly materials**, KISS fosters a culture of sustainability. The institution also integrates these principles into the **curriculum**, educating students on **sustainable consumption practices** that they can implement both on campus and in their communities.

13. Goal 13: Climate Action

At **KISS, climate change** is a key focus area in the **environmental education curriculum**. Students are taught about the causes and consequences of **climate change** and are encouraged to actively participate in **climate action** initiatives. Through **workshops, awareness programs**, and **tree planting campaigns**, KISS instills a sense of responsibility in students to combat environmental degradation and promote **sustainable practices** that help mitigate **climate change**.

14. Goal 14: Life Below Water

KISS incorporates lessons on **marine conservation** and the **importance of aquatic biodiversity** into its environmental education programs. Through **workshops, field visits**, and **educational campaigns**, students learn about the delicate ecosystems in **water bodies** and the critical need to protect them from pollution and over-exploitation. By focusing on **sustainable fishing practices** and **ocean conservation**, KISS helps students become stewards of the world's marine resources.

15. Goal 15: Life on Land

As part of its commitment to **environmental sustainability**, KISS organizes **tree plantation drives, biodiversity conservation programs**, and **ecological awareness campaigns**. These initiatives not only contribute to the **preservation of ecosystems** but also encourage students to actively participate in creating a **greener, more sustainable environment**. Through these programs, students are taught the importance of **conserving wildlife, protecting forests**, and maintaining **biodiversity** for the future.

16. Goal 16: Peace, Justice, and Strong Institutions

KISS emphasizes **value-based education** that nurtures qualities such as **peace, justice**, and **ethical leadership**. Through its **holistic curriculum**, students are taught to uphold principles of **fairness**, **equality**, and **social justice**. By encouraging dialogue, **conflict resolution skills**, and community engagement, **KISS** cultivates a culture of **peace** and **respect**, preparing students to become leaders who will work towards a just and harmonious society.

17. Goal 17: Partnerships for the Goals

KISS works in collaboration with **national and international organizations**, **governments**, and **NGOs** to achieve its educational and developmental goals. By forming strategic partnerships, **KISS** strengthens its impact, sharing knowledge, resources, and best practices to achieve common objectives. These partnerships help **KISS** broaden its reach and contribute to the global efforts toward **sustainable development**, **education**, and **poverty alleviation**.

Prof. Achyuta Samanta's vision aligns seamlessly with the **Sustainable Development Goals (SDGs)**, reflecting his belief in the transformative power of education to create a better world. By addressing all 17 goals through his institutions, he demonstrates how education can serve as the foundation for sustainable development, community empowerment, and global progress.

This comprehensive approach ensures that his work is not just about academic excellence but also about fostering a generation of compassionate, responsible, and capable individuals who can contribute to a more sustainable and equitable future.

Kalinga Institute of Social Science (KISS) (Holistic Education Centre)

Introduction

Education is the birthright of every child, a principle enshrined in Article 21(A) of the Indian Constitution. While this right ensures access to education, achieving universalization of elementary education remains a daunting challenge. Despite significant governmental efforts and financial investment, the goals are often unmet due to **wastage and stagnation**, particularly in tribal and marginalized regions where **multidimensional barriers** persist.

In response to this pressing societal challenge, **Prof. Achyuta Samanta** envisioned and established the **Kalinga Institute of Social Sciences (KISS)**—a beacon of hope and the largest fully free residential educational institution for tribal children in the world. This institution is the **brainchild of a remarkable visionary, philanthropist, social activist, and educationist**, whose life's mission is deeply intertwined with the upliftment of the underprivileged.

KISS was born in 1992-1993, with humble beginnings and a grand vision: to provide **free education, food, accommodation, and healthcare** to the poorest tribal children of India. Starting with just **125 students**, the institution has grown exponentially, reaching an unparalleled strength of over **30,000 students** by the academic year 2015–16. Today, it provides education spanning **KG to Ph.D.**, nurturing generations of tribal children and transforming them into confident, self-reliant, and socially responsible individuals.

For Prof. Samanta, KISS is not just an institution; it is **his life's greatest work (his life time achievement)**, a manifestation of his unshakable belief in education as the most powerful tool for social change. KISS represents his **philosophy of compassion**, inclusion, and empowerment. It reflects his conviction that no child, regardless of their background, should be denied the opportunity to dream and achieve.

KISS's **stellar achievements** are not just in its scale but in its outcomes. It is celebrated globally for managing a **diverse community of 30,000 students under one roof**, providing **world-class facilities**, and achieving **excellence in academics, sports, culture, and social impact**. This institution stands as a testament to how **one man's vision** can break the cycle of poverty, bridge inequalities, and offer a brighter future to generations of tribal children.

The story of KISS is, in essence, the story of **Prof. Achyuta Samanta's heart**—a story of love, resilience, and unwavering dedication to the most vulnerable. It is this deep personal connection that makes KISS not just an educational institution, but a **temple of transformation**, resonating with the hopes and aspirations of tribal children across the country.

Through KISS, **Prof. Samanta has proven that education is not just a right but a lifeline**, one that can lift individuals, families, and entire communities from the depths of deprivation to the pinnacles of success.

Overview of KISS Campus

Kalinga Institute of Social Sciences (KISS) is a preeminent residential educational institution dedicated exclusively to the empowerment of indigenous students. It stands as a unique model of holistic education, integrating academics, skill development, and cultural preservation to create a transformative learning experience.

The expansive KISS campus in Bhubaneswar is composed of an NGO, a school, a college, and a university, each equipped with modern amenities while preserving the essence of indigenous traditions. To ensure a comprehensive and self-sustaining learning environment, KISS is strategically divided into **four specialized campuses**, each with a distinct purpose aligned with the institution's commitment to holistic education:

1. **KISS School Campus** – Focused on foundational education, this campus nurtures young minds with quality schooling, character building, and early skill development.
2. **KISS College Campus** – Dedicated to higher education, this campus offers undergraduate and postgraduate programs that equip students with academic excellence and career-oriented knowledge.
3. **KISS University Campus** – Serving as a hub for advanced learning and research, this campus fosters innovation, leadership, and global academic exposure for indigenous students.
4. **KISS NGO & Vocational Training Campus** – Committed to sustainable livelihood development, this campus provides vocational training, entrepreneurship programs, and community outreach initiatives to enhance self-reliance among students.

KISS is more than just an educational institution—it is a movement towards social transformation. By integrating **education, skill development, sports, and cultural enrichment** in a **green, eco-friendly environment**, KISS empowers indigenous students to realize their full potential and become agents of change in their communities.

KISS Campus – 1:
Foundation of Excellence

Built-up Area: 5,40,000 Sq.ft

KISS Campus – 1 serves as the **core foundation** of the institution, dedicated to **administration, academics, and student welfare**. Designed to accommodate large numbers of students while maintaining a structured and holistic learning environment, this campus is a **self-sufficient educational hub** equipped with modern facilities.

This **eco-friendly** and **technologically advanced** campus embodies the commitment of KISS to providing a **world-class education** while **nurturing indigenous identity, knowledge, and aspirations**.

KISS Campus – 2:
Sports, Vocational Training, and Residential Excellence

Built-up Area: 7,25,000 Sq.ft

KISS Campus – 2 is dedicated to providing a well-rounded educational

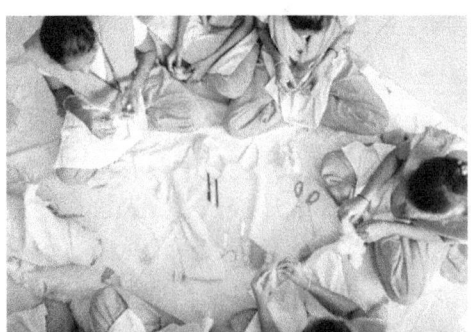

experience with a special focus on **vocational training, sports development**, and **residential facilities**. The campus is designed to equip students with essential life skills while offering modern amenities for both academic and extracurricular growth.

This campus offers a **balanced blend of academics, vocational training, and sports**, creating a dynamic environment for holistic student development. It ensures that every student is empowered with the skills, physical fitness, and values necessary to lead a successful and meaningful life.

KISS Campus – 3:
Academic Excellence and Student Welfare

Built-up Area: 3,00,000 Sq.ft

KISS Campus – 3 is focused on providing a **comprehensive academic environment** while ensuring that student welfare is prioritized. This campus is designed to foster intellectual growth, scientific exploration, and personal development, offering essential amenities for both learning and living.

This campus is designed to foster **academic rigor, scientific curiosity**, and **student care**, ensuring that every student has the opportunity to thrive both academically and personally. It represents KISS's commitment to providing a **well-rounded education** while maintaining a **sustainable and eco-friendly environment**.

KISS Campus – 4:
Higher Education and Student Development

Built-up Area: 4,00,000 Sq.ft

KISS Campus – 4 is dedicated to **higher education**, designed to provide **advanced academic programs** and **comprehensive student support services**. This campus combines modern infrastructure with a strong emphasis on **academic excellence** and **student welfare**, ensuring that every student receives the best environment for their educational and personal growth.

This campus provides a **holistic educational environment**, offering students the resources and facilities they need to thrive academically and personally. The integration of **higher education, student welfare**, and **athletic development** makes Campus – 4 a hub for **academic excellence** and **overall growth**.

Satellite Centres: Expanding Horizons for Education and Service to Mankind

The remarkable success of the **KISS model** in Bhubaneswar, both in terms of **sustainability** and **impact**, has inspired the management to replicate this model in different districts of Odisha and beyond, bringing formal education closer to the marginalized and underserved communities. **KISS** is driven by the vision of **Prof. Achyuta Samanta** to serve humanity and offer **access to quality education** to every child, reflecting the core philosophy of **service to mankind as service to God**.

In addition to **KISS-Delhi**, which operates in collaboration with the **Government of Delhi**, KISS has expanded its footprint to several districts in Odisha, including **Baripada, Balangir, Kalahandi**, and **Balasore**, where it continues to impact thousands of lives by providing **free education, meals,** and lodging. The establishment of these satellite centres ensures that children from tribal and rural areas have the opportunity to thrive in a safe, nurturing, and world-class educational environment.

Furthermore, the vision of **Prof. Achyuta Samanta** extends beyond Indian borders. The KISS family is expanding globally with **five more satellite centres** in the pipeline: **Kandhamal** and **Keonjhar** in Odisha, one in **Maharashtra**, and two in **Bangladesh**. Through these efforts, KISS is bringing the transformative power of education to the most remote corners of the world, making a significant contribution to global development.

These satellite centres are a testament to **KISS's dedication to service** and **global outreach**, striving to make the world a better place by empowering children with education and values that uplift society. With each new center, **Prof. Achyuta Samanta** and KISS continue to realize the mission of **service to mankind** and **service to God**, providing children the opportunities they deserve to lead meaningful, prosperous lives.

KISS Satellite Centre – Bankisole, Mayurbhanj

Location: Bankisole, Mayurbhanj
Inauguration: 9th January 2020
Collaboration: Adani Foundation
Capacity: 1200 girl students
Academics: Class I to Class X, affiliated to Board of Secondary Education, Odisha
Area: Approximately 40 acres
Model: Fully Free Residential School

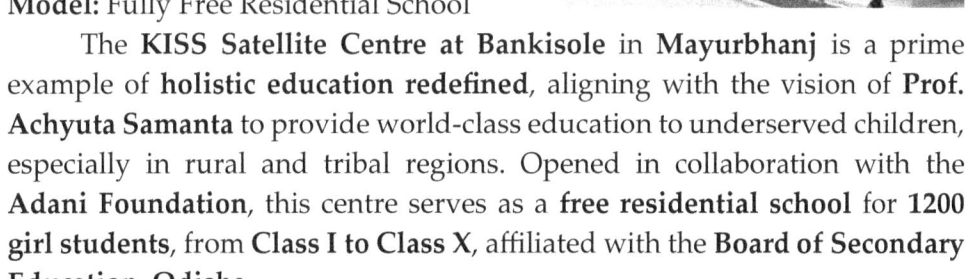

The **KISS Satellite Centre at Bankisole** in **Mayurbhanj** is a prime example of **holistic education redefined**, aligning with the vision of **Prof. Achyuta Samanta** to provide world-class education to underserved children, especially in rural and tribal regions. Opened in collaboration with the **Adani Foundation**, this centre serves as a **free residential school** for **1200 girl students**, from **Class I to Class X**, affiliated with the **Board of Secondary Education, Odisha**.

The **KISS Bankisole Satellite Centre** stands as a testament to the **vision of holistic education**, blending world-class facilities, environmental sustainability, and comprehensive student development in every facet of its design. By offering **free education**, **vocational training**, **sports**, and **healthcare**, KISS continues to redefine the **impact of education** on marginalized communities and empowers students to create a brighter future for themselves and their communities.

KISS Satellite Centre – Rajib Nagar, Balangir

Location: Rajib Nagar, Balangir
Inauguration: 15th February 2020
Collaboration: Motilal Oswal Foundation
Capacity: 1200 girl students
Academics: Class I to Class X, affiliated to Board of Secondary Education, Odisha
Area: Approximately 12 acres
Model: Fully Free Residential School

The **KISS Satellite Centre at Rajib Nagar, Balangir** is a shining example of **Prof. Achyuta Samanta's commitment** to **transforming the lives of tribal children** through **holistic education**. Inaugurated on **15th February 2020**, this centre was established in **collaboration with the Motilal Oswal Foundation**, marking another significant step in his mission to provide **quality education** to children in every corner of **Odisha, India**, and even beyond. Prof. Samanta's deep concern for the **tribal communities**, and his unwavering dedication to uplifting them, is reflected in every aspect of the centre, where every effort is made to ensure that these children receive an **education that nurtures their intellect, character, and physical well-being**.

The **Rajib Nagar centre** serves **1200 girl students**, offering **free residential education** from **Class I to Class X**, affiliated with the **Board of Secondary Education, Odisha**. Set amidst the **scenic serenity of Balangir**, the campus spans **approximately 12 acres** and is designed to provide **world-class facilities** while maintaining the essence of indigenous values.

Prof. **Achyuta Samanta's heart beats for the holistic education** of tribal children in every corner of Odisha, across India, and globally. His vision is to **ensure that these children are equipped with the tools and resources** to overcome the challenges they face and create a brighter future for themselves and their communities. Through his tireless efforts and unwavering dedication, KISS continues to make **quality education** accessible to the most marginalized, demonstrating that when education is provided with love, care, and sustainability, it transforms lives and uplifts societies.

KISS Satellite Centre – Balasore

Location: Balasore
Inauguration: 14th June 2022
Collaboration: Emami Group
Capacity: 1200 girl students
Academics: Class I to Class X, Affiliated to Central Board of Secondary Education (CBSE), Govt. of India
Area: Approximately 12 acres
Model: Fully Free Residential School

The **KISS Satellite Centre at Balasore** stands as a beacon of hope and opportunity for tribal girls, offering a world-class education and nurturing environment in the heart of **Balasore**. Inaugurated on **14th June 2022** in collaboration with the **Emami Group**, this centre is a significant milestone in **Prof. Achyuta Samanta's** mission to uplift the lives of marginalized communities through education. The campus is dedicated to **1200 girl students**, offering **free residential education** from **Class I to Class X**, affiliated with the prestigious **Central Board of Secondary Education (CBSE), Govt. of India**.

Spanning an area of approximately **12 acres**, the **KISS Balasore Centre** is equipped with state-of-the-art facilities that reflect the institution's commitment to providing holistic education. With a focus on **academic excellence**, **personal growth**, and **sustainable development**, the centre offers a nurturing environment for students to thrive in every aspect of life.

The **KISS Balasore Centre** embodies **Prof. Achyuta Samanta's vision** of **holistic education** for tribal children. By offering free education, state-of-the-art facilities, and a commitment to sustainable practices, this centre continues to transform lives and empower the next generation of leaders. Through his visionary leadership, KISS is creating a world where every child, regardless of their background, has access to the tools and opportunities to succeed and contribute meaningfully to society.

KISS Satellite Centre – Bhawanipatna, Kalahandi: Nurturing the Future of Tribal Girls

Location: Bhawanipatna, Kalahandi
Inauguration: 17th June 2022
Capacity: 1200 girl students
Academics: Class I to Class X, Affiliated to Board of Secondary Education, Odisha
Area: Approximately 12 acres
Model: Fully Free Residential School

The **KISS Satellite Centre at Bhawanipatna** in **Kalahandi** is an embodiment of Prof. **Achyuta Samanta's** deep commitment to providing **quality education** to **tribal girls** in the most remote regions of **Odisha**.

Inaugurated on **17th June 2022**, this centre stands as a testament to his vision of **holistic education** that equips tribal children with not just academic knowledge but life skills, physical fitness, and sustainability practices. The centre is a **fully free residential school**, dedicated to serving **1200 girl students** from **Class I to Class X**, affiliated with the **Board of Secondary Education, Odisha**.

Spanning over an area of **12 acres**, the **Bhawanipatna campus** is designed to provide world-class facilities that integrate **modern education** with a focus on **holistic development**. The campus is a blend of **academic excellence**, **vocational skills**, and **eco-conscious practices**, ensuring the well-being and future success of every student.

The **KISS Bhawanipatna Centre** represents the relentless efforts of **Prof. Achyuta Samanta** in transforming the lives of tribal children. Through **free education**, **world-class facilities**, and **sustainability practices**, this centre contributes to the overall development of students, preparing them for leadership and success in all aspects of life. By creating an environment where academic, physical, and personal growth are equally prioritized, **KISS Bhawanipatna** is empowering the next generation of tribal leaders and visionaries.

KISS Delhi: A Beacon of Hope for Underprivileged Children

Location: Delhi, India
Inauguration: 2013
Student Strength: 1200
Academics: Class I to Class X, Central Board of Secondary Education (CBSE), Govt. of India
Area: 15 acres
Model: Fully Free Residential Co-Education Institution

KISS Delhi is a public service-oriented, non-profit initiative founded as a joint venture between the **Government of NCT of Delhi** and **Kalinga Institute of Social Sciences (KISS)**, Bhubaneswar, Odisha. It follows the highly successful **KISS model of education**, which provides **fully free formal education** in a **residential environment**. This model has garnered global recognition for its ability to **eradicate poverty through education** for underprivileged children, becoming a beacon of hope for many.

The institution is the realization of **Dr. Achyuta Samanta's** lifelong mission to provide **underprivileged children** with a **level playing field**. Having experienced poverty firsthand after the loss of his father at the age of 4, Dr. Samanta was determined to create a space where children, regardless of their socio-economic background, could receive a world-class education and have their basic needs met.

Since its inception in **2013**, **KISS Delhi** has been providing **free education, meals, clothing**, and **healthcare** to **1200 children**, breaking the cycle of poverty and offering a brighter future to those who need it the most. Through its world-class facilities and commitment to **holistic education**, **KISS Delhi** is empowering children to overcome their circumstances and build a better life.

Global Footprint: Dr. Samanta's Heartfelt Mission for Tribal Upliftment

Over the years, **KISS** has become more than just an institution – it has emerged as a **beacon of hope** for thousands of children from marginalized communities who face numerous socio-economic challenges. At KISS, these children receive not just **quality education**, but also **food, clothing,** and **healthcare**, ensuring they are nurtured in every aspect of life, enabling them to grow, learn, and thrive in a supportive and holistic environment.

One of the most inspiring aspects of **KISS** is its **global footprint**, which reflects the universal appeal and relevance of its mission. The institution's transformative model has not only **changed lives** in India but has also **inspired** global leaders to replicate its success elsewhere.

Dr. Achyuta Samanta's deep passion and dedication for the **upliftment of tribal children** have been the driving force behind this global expansion. His heart beats for these children, understanding that education is the key to breaking the cycle of poverty and giving them a better future. His vision has reached far beyond the borders of India, touching lives in **Bangladesh, Sri Lanka,** and **Nepal**.

A powerful testament to the global impact of KISS is the story of **Dr. Sabur Khan**, the founder of **Daffodil International University** in **Bangladesh**. After visiting **KISS Bhubaneswar**, he was deeply moved by Dr. Samanta's unwavering commitment to **tribal children's education**. So inspired was he that he invited Dr. Samanta to help establish a similar institution in Bangladesh, **Daffodil Institute of Social Sciences (DISS)**, with KISS offering technical expertise while **Daffodil University** would provide financial support. This collaboration will ensure that children in **Dhaka**, too, have access to the same transformative opportunities as those at KISS.

This ripple effect continues as **KISS** expands to **Jessore, Bangladesh**, and other parts of **South Asia**, including **Sri Lanka** and **Nepal**, ensuring **tribal children** everywhere can experience a better, **holistic education** that empowers them to shape their own futures.

Dr. Samanta's journey from humble beginnings to creating a movement that spans continents is a powerful reminder of the difference one person can make. His commitment to the **upliftment of underprivileged children**, especially **tribal communities**, is a legacy that will continue to **transform lives** across the world, ensuring that **no child** is left behind in the pursuit of education and empowerment.

Dream of Education: The Journey of Kalinga Institute of Social Sciences (KISS)

When the **Kalinga Institute of Social Sciences (KISS)** began its journey in 1992-1993, it started humbly with just **125 tribal children**. Yet, in less than two decades, it has grown into a **global beacon of hope**—the **world's largest residential institute for tribal children**. From its roots in Bhubaneswar, Odisha, KISS has transformed lives, giving the most underprivileged children an opportunity to access **free, high-quality education** and paving the way for a brighter future.

For Odisha's tribal communities, KISS is not just an institution; it is a **lifeline of hope and empowerment**. Thousands of families have witnessed the profound change education can bring, seeing their children excel academically and socially through a unique model that encompasses everything from **kindergarten to postgraduate studies**—a concept fondly referred to by **Prof. Achyuta Samanta** as **"KG to PG."** Prof. Samanta has proven that noble dreams, when backed by passion and perseverance, can achieve what once seemed impossible.

Today, KISS is home to over **30,000 tribal children**, representing **62 different tribes**, including some of India's most vulnerable tribal groups. Remarkably, **60% of the students are girls**, showcasing Prof. Samanta's

dedication to **gender equality and women's empowerment**. The sprawling **84-acre campus**, with a built-up area exceeding near about **2 million square feet**, is a haven where education, health, and well-being come together. Its **15,000-square-foot library**, housing over **40,000 titles**, stands as a symbol of knowledge and opportunity.

KISS offers a **complete package of support**—free **accommodation, meals, healthcare, education**, and even **vocational training**, ensuring that students not only dream but also achieve. To complement this, KISS guarantees **job assurance** upon the completion of education, providing students with a pathway to sustainable livelihoods. This holistic approach ensures that while tribal children embrace the benefits of modern education, they remain rooted in their **cultural heritage**. Prof. Samanta has always emphasized the importance of **preserving tribal identity**, stating, "**We want them to become agents of change in their community while never losing sight of their roots.**"

KISS's mission is rooted in the belief that **education is the most powerful weapon to eradicate poverty and hunger**. It seeks to:
- **Empower tribal children** to compete in the mainstream.
- Enable them to lead **dignified lives** on par with non-tribal counterparts.
- Nurture them as **agents of change**, who can uplift their communities and families.
- Provide **holistic development** through a blend of modern education and cultural preservation.

The institution's influence extends far beyond its campus. KISS has partnered with several globally renowned organizations such as **UNICEF, UNESCO, Oracle Educational Foundation**, and the **Tata Institute of Social Sciences (TISS)**. These collaborations reflect the **worldwide recognition of KISS's mission** and its innovative educational model.

Prof. Samanta's philosophy of education combines **modernity with tradition, innovation with empathy, and global outreach with local relevance**. The holistic education system at KISS is an **integrated approach**, covering not only academic excellence but also life skills, character building, and self-reliance. It redefines education as a tool for social transformation, ensuring that tribal children are **not just educated but truly empowered** to lead their communities toward progress and prosperity.

Through KISS, **Prof. Samanta's dream of education** has become a **living reality**—an extraordinary journey where every child matters, every dream is nurtured, and every success is celebrated as a victory for humanity.

For **Prof. Samanta**, the students of KISS are not merely learners—they are **divine embodiments of hope and potential**, each carrying the spark of a brighter future. In his vision, the sprawling campus of KISS is a **sacred temple**, where every teacher, staff member, and even Prof. Samanta himself serve as **dedicated priests**, committed to nurturing these young souls with boundless care and devotion. The teachers at KISS go beyond the roles of educators; they become **mentors, guardians, and guiding lights**, ensuring that every child feels valued, loved, and empowered. This selfless dedication creates an environment where students not only receive knowledge but also **imbibe values, confidence, and a sense of purpose**.

In this temple of transformation, every small success of the children is celebrated like a divine offering, and every challenge they face is met with unwavering support and compassion. Prof. Samanta believes that serving these children is akin to **serving humanity**, and this ethos inspires everyone at KISS to work tirelessly, day and night, to ensure that no child is left behind. This profound sense of dedication and reverence transforms the KISS community into a **sanctuary of hope**, where the dreams of tribal children take flight, blessed by the collective efforts of their devoted caretakers.

KISS: A Global Beacon of Hope and Equality for Tribal Children -journey continuing...

KISS is not just an institution in Odisha; it has become a **nationwide and global movement** for the upliftment of tribal children. Under the visionary leadership of **Prof. Achyuta Samanta**, KISS has grown far beyond its roots, with branches not just across **India**, but also reaching the hearts of **tribal children in various parts of the world**. Prof. Samanta's dream of **mainstreaming and educating every tribal child in an equal and equitable way** has now extended beyond the confines of a single campus to include **tribal communities from all corners of India**—from the remote hills of the Northeast to the dense forests of Central India. The expansion of KISS to **different campuses in Odisha, India, and abroad** serves as a beacon of hope for tribal communities that have long been left behind, overlooked, and underprivileged in a society that has so often failed to address their needs.

For **Prof. Samanta**, this mission is deeply personal. He recalls the pain of his own childhood, witnessing the hardships and discrimination faced by the **indigenous people**, who for generations have been labeled as "tribal," "Adivasi," "marginalized," and "deprived." These labels have often led to **their exclusion from mainstream opportunities**, trapping them in cycles of poverty and illiteracy. Prof. Samanta's heart ached at the thought that these children, born into such circumstances, would be denied the education and opportunities they deserved simply because of their birth. That injustice ignited his lifelong passion for **equitable education and holistic development**, where no child would be left behind due to the circumstances of their birth.

Through KISS, he has not only **provided access to education**, but has also nurtured **life skills**, instilled **confidence**, and empowered these children to be **agents of change** in their own communities. In a world where society and government have often shown unwillingness or indifference to the plight of the tribal people, Prof. Samanta stood alone in his commitment to **change the narrative**. He took on the **responsibility** that society and the state had long neglected, opening the doors to a future where tribal children are seen not as marginalized, but as **future leaders, innovators, and ambassadors of change**.

KISS is Prof. Samanta's **heartfelt response to the injustice** of an unequal society. It is his **legacy of love and determination**, where every child—regardless of their background—is given the opportunity to thrive. His work continues to heal the wounds of generations and break the chains of discrimination, giving every tribal child a chance to dream and succeed. As KISS grows, so too does the fulfillment of Prof. Samanta's dream, where tribal children are not just educated, but uplifted with dignity, equality, and a sense of belonging in the world. His dedication has turned KISS into a **global symbol of hope and transformation**, where **every child is a promise of a better tomorrow**.

Concept of Holistic Education

The term **holism**, as introduced by **Jan Smuts**, is derived from the Greek word **"holos"**, (ολοσ) which means **"whole"** or **"entire"**. Smuts explains that **holism** is the idea that systems and their properties should be viewed as wholes, not just as a collection of parts. In his book *"Holism and Evolution"*, Smuts argues that **holism** emphasizes the interconnectedness of all elements within a system, whether it be in nature, society, or human beings.

This concept is foundational to **holistic education**, which seeks to nurture the **whole individual**—intellectually, emotionally, socially, and spiritually. Instead of focusing solely on academic achievement, holistic education acknowledges the importance of developing emotional intelligence, ethical values, and practical skills. It recognizes that human beings are dynamic and interconnected, and thus, education should address the full spectrum of a student's growth, fostering a balanced and comprehensive approach to learning. Holistic education, therefore, integrates knowledge, values, and skills to create well-rounded individuals who are capable of contributing meaningfully to society and adapting to an ever-changing world.

Meaning of Holistic Education

Holistic education is an approach that focuses on the overall development of a learner by addressing their intellectual, emotional, social, physical, and spiritual dimensions. It goes beyond traditional academics to ensure that individuals grow as well-rounded human beings capable of critical thinking, empathy, and practical action.

The core idea of holistic education is to nurture the **"whole child"**, integrating knowledge, values, and skills to prepare them for life, not just exams. It emphasizes the interconnectedness of various aspects of learning and life, fostering creativity, emotional well-being, social responsibility, and ethical awareness.

Holistic education often incorporates:
1. **Cognitive development (Head):** Building knowledge and critical thinking skills.
2. **Emotional and ethical growth (Heart):** Encouraging compassion, empathy, and values.
3. **Practical application (Hand):** Focusing on skills, actions, and real-world problem-solving.

By blending these dimensions, holistic education creates lifelong learners who are not only academically competent but also capable of contributing meaningfully to society. This approach is especially important in a world that values emotional intelligence, cultural awareness, and adaptability alongside intellectual achievement.

According to **Prof. Samanta**, **holistic education** is a transformative approach that goes beyond academic success. It is an education system that fulfills all the necessities of students, preparing them not just to excel in academics but to navigate the complexities of life within society as a whole. Prof. Samanta believes that true education helps students **find their identity and purpose** by fostering connections with the community, nature, and humanitarian values. It nurtures a sense of **social awareness, creativity, and responsibility**, empowering students to thrive in a rapidly changing world.

Holistic education, as envisioned by Prof. Samanta, aims to ignite an **intrinsic reverence for life** and inspire a **passionate love for learning**. It is not merely about imparting knowledge but about shaping well-rounded individuals who are empowered to:

- **Know themselves** and embrace their unique identities.
- Foster **healthy relationships** and exhibit pro-social behavior.
- Achieve **social, emotional, aesthetic, and cultural development**.
- Build resilience and innovation to tackle challenges with courage and creativity.

Prof. Samanta's philosophy stems from his deep concern for the **tribal communities** he has dedicated his life to serving. He observed that academic knowledge alone was insufficient to overcome the **hurdles of modern society**, especially for the tribal youth, who often face unemployment, social exclusion, and even fall prey to **Maoist influences** due to a lack of opportunities and necessary life skills. He realized that the **existing education system failed to address the unique needs** of tribal children, leaving them vulnerable and disconnected from mainstream society.

To address this **crisis of inclusion and empowerment**, Prof. Samanta introduced the concept of holistic education through the **Kalinga Institute of Social Sciences (KISS)**. This visionary model is designed to be a **panacea for the challenges faced by vulnerable tribal communities**, equipping children with not only academic knowledge but also life skills, values, and self-confidence. By doing so, KISS aims to ensure that these children not only **enter mainstream society** but do so with dignity, self-reliance, and a sense of purpose.

Holistic education at KISS is not just a philosophy; it is a **living reality** that has touched the lives of thousands. It is a beacon of hope for tribal children, offering them a chance to **dream, grow, and lead a fulfilling life**, free from the barriers that have historically held their communities back. As **Prof. Shantha Sinha**, Chairperson of the National Commission for Protection of Child Rights, aptly said, *"We have been dreaming of providing education to tribal children for long. KISS is the solution."*

Through this approach, Prof. Samanta has proven that education is not just about academic achievements but about building a better world—one where **every child, regardless of their background, can live a life of purpose, dignity, and endless possibilities**.

Prof. Samants's Holistic Education: Blending the 3 H's, 3 R's, and 3 E's

Prof. Achyuta Samanta's vision of holistic education at KISS is deeply rooted in the development of the **3 H's—Head, Heart, and Hand**, creating a balanced individual through intellectual growth, emotional well-being, and practical skills. Simultaneously, the **3 R's—Reading, Writing, and Arithmetic** form the academic foundation essential for cognitive development and lifelong learning. Beyond academics, the **3 E's—Educate, Empower, and Enable** highlight the transformative role of education in uplifting marginalized communities, particularly tribal students, by equipping them with knowledge, confidence, and opportunities for self-reliance. This comprehensive approach integrates intellectual, moral, and practical dimensions, ensuring that education at KISS is not merely about literacy but about nurturing responsible, skilled, and empowered individuals. By harmonizing these elements, holistic education becomes a powerful tool for breaking cycles of poverty and fostering sustainable development, ultimately shaping future leaders and change-makers.

Philosophical Foundations of Holism in Education: Achyuta Samanta's Perspective (Metaphysics, Epistemology, and Axiology)

Achyuta Samanta's vision of **Holism in Education** is deeply rooted in **Metaphysics (Reality), Epistemology (Knowledge), and Axiology (Values & Ethics)**. His educational philosophy, as implemented in **Kalinga Institute of Social Sciences (KISS)**, emphasizes the **integration of intellectual, emotional, social, cultural, physical, and spiritual development** to nurture self-sufficient, socially responsible, and empowered individuals.

1. Metaphysics (Reality): Understanding the Whole Person

Prof. Achyuta Samanta's metaphysical perspective sees reality **as holistic and interconnected**, where individuals are part of a larger social, **cultural, and environmental whole.** Education, in this view, must nurture all aspects of the human experience—**intellectual, emotional, practical, and ethical**—fostering harmony between the self and society.

He believes that **true existence is inclusive**, and **education must be a transformativeforce** that uplifts individuals from all backgrounds, especially the **marginalized**. Every person deserves **equal opportunities for growth**, regardless of socio-economic status.

Key Concepts:
- **Interconnectedness**: The belief that everything in life is interconnected, and therefore, education should nurture **the complete human ex-**

perience, encompassing emotional, intellectual, and practical growth.
- **Unity in Diversity**: Recognizing the **diversity of human experiences**, Prof. Samanta advocates for an education system that respects **cultural, social, and individual diversity**, while fostering a shared sense of **community and social responsibility**.
- **Holistic Reality**: Prof. Samanta emphasizes the reality of **human beings as whole, multidimensional individuals** who must be educated beyond the confines of academics to embrace **empathy, emotional intelligence, and ethical values**.

Core Belief: "Education as a Unifying Force of Existence"
- Reality is **not fragmented** into academic and non-academic aspects—**everything in life is interconnected**.
- Education should **bridge the gap between social classes**, enabling holistic well-being and sustainable development.
- The purpose of education is **not just to survive but to thrive**, focusing on **self-actualization and community upliftment**.

The 3H's Model in Metaphysics (Head, Heart, Hands):
- **Head (Intellectual Development)** – Holistic education should nurture critical thinking, reasoning, and problem-solving.
- **Heart (Emotional & Social Development)** – Learning must cultivate compassion, empathy, and human dignity.
- **Hands (Practical & Skill-based Development)** – Education must provide life skills, 21st-century competencies, and self-employment opportunities.

Example: Implementation in KISS

At **KISS**, education is **not just about literacy** but about **nurturing entire human potential**—students receive **academic knowledge, vocational training, moral education, sports training, and cultural exposure**, ensuring their holistic development.

2. Epistemology (Knowledge): Holistic Learning and Development

Prof. Achyuta Samanta envisions knowledge as multidimensional (**that values multiple forms of knowledge and ways of knowing**), integrating academic excellence, practical skills, emotional intelligence, and ethical awareness. His epistemological approach promotes **learner-centered, experience-based education** that empowers students to become **self-reliant and future-ready**. He believes that education must go beyond bookish learning, embracing **real-world application**, critical thinking, and personal growth. In this holistic framework, knowledge is not fragmented but interconnected—blending the cognitive, emotional, and social aspects of learning to foster well-rounded individuals.

Key Concepts:
- **Integrated Knowledge**: Knowledge should not be seen as fragmented but as an interconnected whole. Academic learning (the 3Rs—Reading, Writing, and Arithmetic) should be integrated with emotional (the 3Hs—Head, Hand, and Heart) and ethical dimensions (the 3Es—Educate, Empower, Enable) to form a well-rounded approach to learning.
- **Experiential Learning**: Knowledge is acquired not only through formal education but also through experience. Prof. Samanta's educational philosophy emphasizes **hands-on, real-world learning,** where students engage with their environment, reflect on their experiences, and gain wisdom.
- **Empathy and Emotional Intelligence**: Knowledge should encompass more than intellectual comprehension; it should include **emotional intelligence** and the ability to empathize, solve social issues, and act with **compassion.**

Core Belief: *"Knowledge Should Educate, Empower, and Enable"*
- Knowledge must be **experiential and practical**, not just theoretical.
- Learning should focus on **self-sufficiency, employment, and entrepreneurship** rather than mere memorization.
- Education must include **scientific reasoning, cultural wisdom, ethical awareness, and vocational expertise**.

The 3R's Model in Epistemology (Reading, Writing, Arithmetic):
- **Reading** – Enhancing comprehension, critical analysis, and knowledge acquisition.
  Writing – Strengthening communication, self-expression, and intellectual creativity.
  Arithmetic – Developing logical reasoning, problem-solving, and quantitative skills.
- **The 3E's Model in Epistemology (Educate, Empower, Enable):**
- **Educate** – Provide quality academic knowledge integrated with cultural and ethical learning.
  Empower – Equip students with **life skills, entrepreneurship training, and vocational education** for real-world success.
- **Enable** – Ensure students become **self-sufficient and contribute meaningfully to society**.
- **Example: Implementation in KISS**
  - **Skill-based education** ensures that students are job-ready, promoting

self-employment and entrepreneurship.
- **Technology-integrated learning** at KIIT ensures that students are prepared for the **digital and global economy**.
- **Multidisciplinary knowledge approach** allows students to develop **scientific, technical, cultural, and ethical competencies** simultaneously.

3. Axiology (Values & Ethics): The Ethical Imperative in Education

For Prof. Achyuta Samanta, **education is incomplete without moral and ethical grounding**. He emphasizes that education must not only impart knowledge and skills but also cultivate **gratitude, empathy, compassion, honesty**, and **integrity**. His **holistic education model** is deeply rooted in **service, social justice, and sustainable development**, aiming to shape responsible citizens who actively contribute to the well-being of society. Prof. Samanta views education as a **moral endeavour**, where values are not supplementary but central to the formation of individuals capable of driving meaningful social change.

Key Concepts:
- **Value-Based Education:** Education must go beyond the academic curriculum and instill in students a strong ethical foundation. This includes fostering **empathy, social responsibility**, and the recognition of the interconnectedness of all human beings.
- **Ethical Leadership:** Education should prepare students to take on leadership roles in society with a strong sense of **moral responsibility**. Students should be taught to make decisions based on values like **fairness, justice, and sustainability**.
- **Empowerment Through Values:** Prof. Samanta believes that values are not just ideals but essential tools for **empowerment.** By fostering values, students are empowered to make choices that improve their lives and contribute to societal progress.

Core Belief: *"Education for Ethical Leadership and Social Transformation"*
- **Moral & Character Education** – Learning must instill integrity, honesty, and ethical decision-making.
- **Emotional Intelligence & Compassion** – Education should promote kindness, teamwork, and social responsibility.
- **Cultural & Spiritual Growth** – Students must be aware of **their cultural roots** while being **open to diversity and global perspectives**.

Integration of 3H's, 3R's, and 3E's in Axiology:
- **3H's (Head, Heart, Hands):** Education should **not only teach** but also **transform individuals into ethical, responsible leaders**.
- **3R's (Reading, Writing, Arithmetic):** Ethical values should be embedded in **academic learning and professional skills**.
- **3E's (Educate, Empower, Enable):** Education must **enable individuals to** uplift their communities, ensuring inclusive growth.

Example: Implementation in KISS
- Social Responsibility – KISS provides **free education, healthcare, and sustainable livelihood** to **tribal students**, ensuring **equity and justice**.
- Holistic Well-being – Education at KISS includes **sports, yoga, meditation, cultural activities, and moral education** to promote **physical and mental well-being**.
- Community Development – KISS graduates actively **engage in social work, leadership, and nation-building**, fulfilling the **true purpose of holistic education**.

Conclusion: Achyuta Samanta as the Father of Holism in 21st-Century Education

- Unlike traditional holistic education models that remained **philosophical and impractical**, Achyuta Samanta's vision **materializes holistic learning in real-world education systems**. He **redefines holistic education** by ensuring that students receive:

The Holistic Education Model envisioned by Prof. Achyuta Samanta integrates academic excellence with values, life skills, and community responsibility, ensuring the all-round development of learners.

- Academic Knowledge + Life Skills + Entrepreneurship + Moral & Ethical Values + Cultural Awareness + Physical & Mental Well-being Sports & Yoga + Sustainable Development + Community Engagement + Leadership Training

Holistic Human Development: A Multidimensional Framework of Growth

Tagline: "*Educating the whole person – mind, body, heart, and spirit.*"

In the educational philosophy of Dr. Achyuta Samanta, holistic human development stands at the core of pedagogical innovation and social transformation. Rooted in his commitment to inclusive and value-based education, this approach aims not just to impart academic excellence, but to cultivate empowered individuals capable of contributing meaningfully to society. It emphasizes the integration of diverse developmental dimensions that shape a human being into a balanced, responsible, and compassionate citizen.

The framework of Holistic Human Development can be visualized as a circular model with ten interrelated and equally significant domains (Samanta's Visualization), each reinforcing the others:

1. Academic Knowledge

Academic learning forms the foundation of cognitive growth. At KISS and similar institutions inspired by this model, structured curricula ensure the mastery of core subjects and 21st-century competencies, enabling learners to compete in global academic and professional arenas.

Example: Students not only study Mathematics or Science but also apply their knowledge in real-life problem-solving activities.

2. Life Skills

Life Skills education equips learners with critical thinking, decision-making, emotional intelligence, and interpersonal abilities. These skills empower students to handle everyday challenges and transitions with confidence and empathy.

Example: Programs supported by UNFPA at KISS help students engage in role-playing activities on topics like peer pressure, time management, and self-awareness.

3. **Entrepreneurship**

An entrepreneurial mindset nurtures innovation, creativity, and self-reliance. Dr. Samanta's model encourages vocational training and exposure to business development, helping students envision pathways of economic independence.

Example: Skill training in areas like tailoring, handicrafts, or digital services is provided along with mentorship on launching micro-enterprises.

4. **Cultural Awareness**

Preserving and promoting indigenous culture is integral to identity formation. Cultural awareness helps students stay rooted while appreciating diversity, fostering mutual respect and heritage pride.
Example: Tribal dances, folklore, and local art forms are embedded in co-curricular activities to ensure cultural continuity.

5. **Sports & Yoga**

Physical development is nurtured through structured physical education, traditional yoga, and competitive sports. These activities promote discipline, resilience, and bodily well-being.

Example: Daily yoga sessions and participation in state and national sports events are mandatory in the residential curriculum of KISS.

6. **Physical & Mental Wellbeing**

A holistic approach cannot ignore the synergy between physical and mental health. Access to nutritious food, healthcare, and psycho-social support systems ensures holistic wellness.

Example: Free health check-ups, counseling units, and mindfulness sessions are integrated into daily routines.

7. **Sustainable Development**

Understanding ecological balance and sustainable living is critical for long-term planetary health. Environmental education is imparted through both theory and practice.
Example: Plantation drives, waste management awareness campaigns, and workshops on water conservation are actively conducted.

8. Community Engagement

Active participation in community welfare nurtures a sense of service and social responsibility. Learners become change agents, committed to improving the conditions of their own and others' communities.

Example: Students take part in village outreach programs, health awareness drives, and disaster relief volunteering.

9. Leadership Training

Leadership is cultivated through democratic participation, mentorship, and experiential learning. The goal is to foster confident, ethical, and inclusive leaders.

Example: Student councils, leadership camps, and public speaking forums are used to groom young leaders.

10. Moral & Ethical Values

Values like compassion, honesty, humility, and justice lie at the heart of holistic education. These are not just taught but lived through institutional culture and role models.

Example: The "Art of Giving" movement led by Dr. Samanta instills a spirit of altruism and universal brotherhood.

In essence, Holistic Human Development is not an adjunct to education—it is education. It aligns seamlessly with the NEP 2020 vision and reflects the lived reality of transformative models like that of KISS. By nurturing every dimension of the learner—academic, emotional, cultural, physical, ethical, and entrepreneurial—Dr. Samanta's vision offers a scalable, inclusive, and sustainable model for future-ready education.

Through **KISS**, he has successfully implemented **Holism in Education** on a **large scale**, proving that **holistic education can uplift marginalized communities, empower individuals, and create future-ready leaders**.

"Achyuta Samanta's HOLISTIC EDUCATION is not just a concept—it is a proven reality that transforms lives."

Aims of Education: A Progressive and Holistic Perspective

In the words of **Brubacher**, *"Progressive education has no fixed aims or values in advance. Educational aims, no matter how well authenticated by the past, are not to be projected indefinitely into the future. In a world rendered precarious and contingent by a compound of the novel and the customary, educational aims must be held subject to revision as one advances into the future. If education has only general* *aims in the light of which successive revisions can take place, it is the pupil's growth. But growth itself has no end beyond further growth. In other words, education is its own end."*

This vision aligns seamlessly with the philosophy of **Prof. Samanta**, a pioneer in progressive and holistic education. Prof. Samanta does not believe in fixed, predetermined, or ultimate aims of education, recognizing that such rigid frameworks often fail to address the dynamic needs of society. Instead, he advocates for a progressive, context-sensitive approach that aligns educational goals with the evolving requirements of individuals and society. His approach emphasizes that education should adapt to the *"need of the hour"* and be rooted in the realities of the present, ensuring its relevance for the future.

Prof. Samanta's largest institution, which embodies these principles, stands as a testament to the belief that **education should not be bound by static ideals but should instead serve as a tool for societal transformation and individual growth**. In his philosophy, the aims of education must remain fluid, reflecting the ever-changing landscape of human development, societal needs, and global progress.

With a holistic lens, Prof. Samanta has identified a few progressive aims of education that resonate deeply with the spirit of our times. These aims include:

1. Service to Mankind

Prof. Achyuta Samanta is a profound lover of humanity, whose heart beats for the poor, downtrodden, ignorant, helpless, and destitute. From an early age, he was deeply moved by their suffering and resolved to dedicate his life to alleviating their pain. For him, true divinity does not reside in worshiping idols within temples but in recognizing and serving the divine in humanity. He passionately advocated the philosophy that **"service to mankind is service to God."**

In his educational philosophy, he emphasizes that education should instill in students the value of serving humanity. He believed that education must go beyond academics; it must nurture the soul, awaken the innate potential within individuals, and cultivate virtues like brotherhood, love, and empathy. These qualities, he argued, are the bedrock of a compassionate society.

Prof. Samanta's vision finds a living embodiment in the activities at **Kalinga Institute of Social Sciences (KISS)**. This institution stands as a beacon of selfless service and holistic education, where over 30,000 tribal children are empowered not just with knowledge but with values that inspire them to uplift their communities.

Practical Example: The KISS Model of Service to Mankind

At KISS, students are not only taught academic subjects but are also actively involved in initiatives that teach them the importance of giving back to society. For instance:

1. **Community Service Projects**: Students participate in community welfare programs such as healthcare camps, literacy drives, and awareness campaigns in remote tribal areas, directly impacting the lives of the marginalized.

2. **Peer-to-Peer Education**: Senior students mentor younger ones, creating a cycle of care and support, mirroring the principle of brotherhood and mutual growth.

3. **Sustainable Development Initiatives**: Students are engaged in activities like planting trees, promoting environmental sustainability, and spreading awareness about climate change, thereby serving both humanity and the planet.

4. **Empathy through Experiential Learning**: Children are exposed to real-world challenges faced by their communities, fostering a deep sense of responsibility and empathy.

One particularly inspiring example is the story of **tribal students from KISS who, after completing their education, return to their villages to serve as teachers, healthcare workers, and community leaders**, bringing transformative change to the lives of thousands. This cycle of empowerment exemplifies how education rooted in service creates a ripple effect of positive change.

Inspirational Tagline by him

"Selfless Service, Boundless Impact—Education for All, Progress for Humanity."

Core Philosophy

Prof. Samanta envisions an education system where every child learns to see humanity as one family and recognizes their responsibility toward others. In his words:

"The purpose of education is not merely to earn a living but to give life meaning by serving others. True education is the one that awakens the divine within and inspires an individual to serve society selflessly. When a child learns to see God in the faces of the poor and marginalized, only then has education fulfilled its purpose."

2. Simple Living and High Thinking

One of the cornerstone principles in **Prof. Achyuta Samanta's educational philosophy** is the ideal of **simple living and high thinking**. This principle is not merely theoretical for him—it is a way of life that he practices every day and encourages among students at KISS.

Prof. Samanta's life is a shining example of this philosophy. Despite founding one of the world's largest tribal education institutions, he lives in a modest two-bedroom house, furnished with just four plastic chairs. While he has invested billions into fulfilling his dream of educating thousands of tribal children, his personal needs remain minimal. This simplicity is a testament to his elevated thinking and unyielding commitment to his mission.

Born into poverty, Prof. Samanta started his journey with just ₹4,000 in a challenging environment, yet his **strong determination and visionary mindset** transformed his humble beginnings into a globally recognized institution. This contrast between his austere personal life and his monumental achievements underscores the essence of "simple living, high thinking."

Key Lessons and Practices at KISS

1. **Modesty in Action**:

    Prof. Samanta's simplicity is reflected in his everyday life. He wears a humble dress pattern—a blue pant and white shirt—and carries a simple Reynolds pen in his pocket. This understated approach is a message to students and staff that greatness lies not in outward appearances but in purpose-driven actions.

2. **Simplicity in Campus Life**:

    At KISS, students are encouraged to adopt simplicity in their daily lives. Extravagance is avoided, and the focus is placed on developing the mind, fostering discipline, and cultivating strong values.

3. **Investing in Minds, Not Luxuries**:

    Resources at KISS are directed toward enhancing education, skills, and personal development rather than unnecessary luxuries. Students learn that success comes from hard work, perseverance, and a clear vision, not material possessions.

4. **Empowering the Marginalized**:
   The institution is a testament to his belief that high thinking can overcome even the most challenging circumstances. By educating and empowering over 30,000 tribal children annually, KISS has become a global example of how simple living can fuel transformative change.

Inspirational Tagline by him

"A life of simplicity, a mind of greatness—education for the soul and society."

"Modest in life, mighty in purpose—empowering through simplicity and vision."

Core Philosophy

At the heart of this philosophy lies the belief that **the mind must be developed, trained, and controlled** to lead a purposeful life. Simplicity in living is not just about material possessions but about aligning one's life with higher ideals and meaningful goals. Prof. Samanta emphasizes that:

1. **True greatness comes from within**: A person's worth is determined by the depth of their thoughts and the strength of their actions, not by their possessions.
2. **Focus on purpose, not appearances**: High thinking requires focusing on long-term impact and meaningful contributions rather than superficial success.
3. **Education as a means to transform lives**: Simplicity in living allows resources and energy to be directed toward empowering others through education, as seen in KISS's transformative impact.

At the heart of this principle lies the conviction that simplicity enhances focus and fosters clarity, while high thinking leads to lasting social impact. For Prof. Samanta, personal austerity is not a sacrifice, but a powerful tool for social change.

In his words:

"True greatness does not reside in possessions but in purpose. When you lead a simple life, your thoughts soar higher. Education must teach students to look beyond material success—to think deeply, act ethically, and live purposefully. Only then does learning become truly transformative."

3. Stress on the Practical Side of Life

Prof. Samanta has always been deeply sensitive to the plight of the millions in India who struggle with poverty, hunger, and deprivation. He firmly believes that ignorance and a lack of awareness are the root causes of this suffering. According to him, education should not only enlighten minds but also empower individuals to face life's challenges with confidence. For Prof. Samanta, the ultimate aim of education is to make individuals self-reliant by equipping them with skills that bear practical utility in their daily lives.

Practical Education for Self-Reliance

In his visionary approach to education, Prof. Samanta emphasizes the importance of vocational training and life skills. He advocates for an education system that prepares individuals not only academically but also practically, enabling them to earn a livelihood and lead a dignified life. This philosophy is reflected in the initiatives at **Kalinga Institute of Social Sciences (KISS)**, where skill development and vocational training form an integral part of the curriculum.

Practical Initiatives at KISS

1. **Skill-Oriented Programs**:

To fulfill his vision, KISS has introduced a wide range of skill-oriented programs aimed at empowering students to sustain themselves in a competitive and struggling society. These include training in:
   - Candle making

- Phenyl and hand wash production
- Perfume creation
- Dish wash and floor cleaner manufacturing
- Pickle and toy making
- Liquid detergent and vehicle wash preparation

These activities instill a sense of confidence and provide students with practical skills they can use to support themselves and their families.

2. **Industrial Sector Collaboration**:

Understanding the demands of the modern workforce, Prof. Samanta has also collaborated with organizations such as the **United Nations, government agencies, and various NGOs** to provide training in industrial and sector-specific skills. These programs are designed to meet the challenges of the present job market and ensure that students are not only trained but also placed in meaningful employment.

3. **Holistic Skill Development**:

Alongside traditional vocational training, students at KISS receive exposure to cutting-edge industrial skills such as:

- Digital literacy and IT training
- Tailoring and embroidery
- Renewable energy projects
- Organic farming and food processing

4. **Placement and Sustainability**:

The comprehensive skill-building initiatives at KISS ensure that students are equipped to secure jobs, start their businesses, or become self-employed, thereby breaking the cycle of poverty and dependence.

Inspirational Tagline by him

"From classrooms to livelihoods—education that builds lives, not just resumes."

Core Philosophy

Prof. Samanta's educational philosophy emphasizes that **education must be life-oriented and transformative**, focusing on practical utility rather than abstract knowledge alone. He believes that:

1. **Education should empower self-reliance**: Every individual should have the ability to stand on their own feet and lead a dignified life.
2. **Practical education transforms lives**: Learning that addresses real-world needs empowers individuals to break free from the shackles of poverty and ignorance.

3. **Collaboration for change is vital**: Partnerships with global and local organizations help bring innovative training and placement opportunities, ensuring sustainable livelihoods.

Prof. Samanta's initiatives at KISS are a living embodiment of his belief that education must address the practical realities of life. By teaching skills like candle making, pickle production, and industrial training, students gain not just knowledge but a pathway to self-reliance. His collaborative efforts with the **United Nations and other organizations** further ensure that education is a stepping stone to a sustainable future.

In Prof. Samanta's words:
"The true purpose of education is to transform lives. It must empower individuals to rise above their circumstances, face challenges with courage, and contribute meaningfully to society."

Through his practical approach to education, Prof. Samanta has set a new benchmark for creating a generation of empowered individuals who are not just educated but are also equipped to thrive in the modern world.

4. Universal Education

Prof. Achyuta Samanta believes that **education is the birthright of every child**, an inalienable right enshrined in Article 21(A) of the Indian Constitution. He is deeply committed to the idea that education should not be confined to a privileged few or remain the monopoly of an elite group. Instead, it must be accessible to all, transcending barriers of caste, creed, color, gender, social status, or region.

Prof. Samanta's philosophy is deeply rooted in the conviction that **universal education is the foundation of an equitable and progressive society**. His lifelong mission is to extend education to those who have been historically marginalized, particularly India's **Scheduled Tribes (STs)**, who represent one of the most vulnerable and underserved groups in the country.
Education for the Marginalized for universal aim of education

Prof. Samanta recognizes that the **Scheduled Tribes**, often left behind in both education and development, require special attention to bridge the gap of inequity. He firmly believes that education is the **only panacea** for breaking the cycles of poverty, discrimination, and exclusion that persist in society.

Through education, Prof. Samanta envisions a society where every child, regardless of their background, realizes the importance of learning. By fostering an inclusive approach to education, he aims to nurture a generation of individuals from all communities who can collectively contribute to the intellectual and developmental growth of the nation.

Initiatives at KISS

The **Kalinga Institute of Social Sciences (KISS)** stands as a testament to Prof. Samanta's vision of universal education. The institution, the largest of its kind in the world, provides **free, quality education** to over 30,000 indigenous students from marginalized backgrounds.

1. **Empowering the Tribal Community**:

KISS has been instrumental in transforming the lives of thousands of tribal students, offering them access to education that was once beyond their reach. The institution provides holistic education—academic, vocational, and cultural—ensuring that these students grow into confident, self-reliant individuals.

2. **Breaking Barriers**:

At KISS, students from diverse tribal backgrounds come together, overcoming centuries of exclusion. The institution's **inclusive environment** fosters unity, equality, and a shared sense of purpose, enabling students to break free from the stereotypes and prejudices that have historically defined their identities.

3. **Cultural Preservation Through Education**:

While integrating tribal students into the mainstream education system, KISS also emphasizes the preservation and promotion of their rich cultural heritage. Students are encouraged to take pride in their traditions while embracing modern education as a tool for empowerment.

4. **Nation-Building Through Universal Education**:

Prof. Samanta's efforts extend beyond just educating individuals. His mission is to create **intellectual parity across all communities**, building a nation where every citizen contributes to its development, regardless of their social or economic background.

Core Philosophy

1. **Education is a Fundamental Right**: Every child deserves access to education, as it is the cornerstone of personal and societal growth.
2. **Inclusive Education for Equality**: Education must bridge the gap between communities, eliminating the disparities caused by caste, creed, and social status.
3. **Empowering the Underserved**: Universal education should prioritize those historically excluded from the mainstream, particularly the most vulnerable communities.

4. **Unity Through Diversity**: By educating all segments of society, we can build a nation that thrives on the collective strength of diverse intellects and talents.

Inspirational Tagline by him
"Education for all, empowerment for generations—bridging divides through universal learning."
In his words:
"Education is not just a privilege; it is the foundation of dignity, equality, and progress. Through education, we can break the barriers that divide us and build a society that thrives on unity and shared prosperity."

Prof. Samanta's commitment to universal education is not merely theoretical—it is lived out daily at KISS, where thousands of tribal students are empowered to rewrite their destinies. His work is a clarion call to the world, reminding us that education is the greatest equalizer and the most powerful tool for transforming lives and societies.

5. All-Round Development of Personality

Prof. Achyuta Samanta's educational philosophy revolves around the **holistic development of the child**. He firmly believes that every child is naturally endowed with a wealth of untapped potential—physical, intellectual, emotional, and spiritual. However, he stresses that for a child to grow into a well-balanced, contributing member of society, this potential must be nurtured **harmoniously**.

Development that is limited to a few aspects of a child's personality is **undesirable**, as it may lead to imbalances and maladjustments, which can hinder their ability to interact meaningfully with society. Prof. Samanta strongly advocates for the **all-round development of the personality**, emphasizing that true education should focus on nurturing the **whole child**—mind, body, spirit, and emotions.

The Core of All-Round Development

Prof. Samanta's vision for education is rooted in the idea that **every aspect of the child's personality must be developed in balance**, including the physical, mental, emotional, spiritual, social, moral, and aesthetic dimensions. To achieve this, he stresses the importance of a comprehensive approach to education that encourages growth in all these areas, not just academic achievement.

1. **Development of 3 H's**:

Prof. Samanta emphasizes the **3 H's—Head, Heart, and Hand**—as the essence of all educational activities. These principles guide students toward achieving mental (head), emotional (heart), and practical (hand) skills. This holistic approach ensures that students are not only intellectually capable but also emotionally intelligent and practically skilled, making them well-rounded individuals.

- **Head (Intellectual Development)**: Cognitive abilities are nurtured through academic learning, critical thinking, and problem-solving exercises.
- **Heart (Emotional and Moral Development)**: Empathy, compassion, love, and moral responsibility are instilled through activities such as community service, group discussions, and cultural experiences.
- **Hand (Practical and Vocational Skills)**: The development of practical skills ensures that students are equipped to meet real-world challenges, fostering a sense of self-reliance and creativity.

2. **Development of 3 R's**:

Prof. Samanta also emphasizes the importance of the **3 R's—Reading, Writing, and Arithmetic**—as foundational components of education. While they serve as critical building blocks of academic learning, these skills should be integrated with life skills and real-world applications for harmonious development.

1. **Foundational Learning:**
   - **Reading** enhances comprehension and opens the door to knowledge across all subjects.
   - **Writing** develops the ability to express thoughts, ideas, and emotions clearly.
   - **Arithmetic** forms the basis of logical thinking, problem-solving, and decision-making.
2. **Integration with Life Skills:**
   - Achyuta Samanta believes these academic skills must go beyond textbooks. For example:
     - Reading should foster critical thinking and cultural awareness.
     - Writing should empower students to communicate effectively in practical situations.
     - Arithmetic should help students manage real-life scenarios like budgeting and planning.
3. **Real-World Applications:**
   - Education must prepare students for **life's practical**

challenges, such as employment, entrepreneurship, and community development.
- By blending the 3 R's with vocational training and skill development, students gain the confidence to face real-world problems and become self-reliant.

4. **Harmonious Development:**
   - Achyuta Samanta's vision ensures that education addresses not only intellectual growth but also social, emotional, and cultural aspects, creating individuals who are prepared for holistic and sustainable progress.

In essence, the 3 R's are the **roots of education**, and their integration with life skills acts as the **bridge to empowerment** and community transformation.

3. **Emphasis on 3E's**

   The **3 E's—Educate, Empower, and Enable**—are central to fostering **holistic education** and resonate with Achyuta Samanta's philosophy of creating well-rounded, self-reliant individuals. These three elements work in harmony to address the intellectual, social, emotional, and practical needs of learners, ensuring their comprehensive development.

1. **Educate**
   - **Core Idea:** Education is the foundation of personal and societal transformation.
   - **Explanation:** Educating individuals equips them with knowledge, critical thinking, and skills essential for intellectual growth. However, it's not just about academics—holistic education also imparts ethical values, cultural awareness, and a sense of responsibility.
   - **Application:** Prof. Samanta's institutions like KISS emphasize accessible, inclusive, and quality education that combines academics with life skills and vocational training.

2. **Empower**
   - **Core Idea:** Empowerment enables individuals to realize their potential and take charge of their lives.
   - **Explanation:** Education alone is incomplete without empowerment. It builds confidence and self-belief, allowing individuals to break free from social and economic barriers. Empowerment focuses on creating opportunities for marginalized communities to participate equally in society.
   - **Application:** Achyuta Samanta empowers students, particularly from

tribal backgrounds, by providing platforms to showcase their talents, access higher education, and achieve financial independence.

3. Enable
- **Core Idea:** Enabling individuals bridges the gap between potential and practical outcomes.
- **Explanation:** Enabling goes beyond empowerment by providing the resources, tools, and support systems needed to succeed. It focuses on practical implementation, helping individuals apply their knowledge and skills effectively in real-world scenarios.
- **Application:** At KISS and KIIT, students are enabled through skill development programs, internships, mentorship, and exposure to employment opportunities, ensuring they can contribute meaningfully to society.

Synergy of the 3 E's
- **Educate** lays the groundwork for knowledge and awareness.
- **Empower** builds the confidence to act on that knowledge.
- **Enable** ensures the capability to transform knowledge and confidence into action.

Holistic Vision
Together, the **3 E's** create individuals who are not only academically sound but also socially responsible, economically independent, and culturally rooted. Achyuta Samanta's philosophy uses these principles to uplift entire communities, particularly marginalized groups, through education that is transformative and inclusive.

Comprehensive Model of All-Round & Holistic Development
Together, the **3 E's (Educate, Empower, Enable)**, **3 R's (Reading, Writing, Arithmetic)**, and **3 H's (Head, Heart, Hand)** work in synergy to create individuals who are academically sound, socially responsible, economically independent, and culturally rooted.
Achyuta Samanta's philosophy integrates these principles to provide a well-rounded education that uplifts not just individuals but entire communities, particularly marginalized groups, through a transformative and inclusive approach.

- **3 E's** ensure that individuals gain knowledge (**Educate**), develop self-confidence to act (**Empower**), and acquire the tools to succeed in real-life scenarios (**Enable**).

- **3 R's** provide the foundational skills of **Reading, Writing,** and **Arithmetic**, which are essential for intellectual development and practical problem-solving.
- **3 H's** balance the use of the **Head (intellect), Heart (compassion and values)**, and **Hand (skills and action)** to cultivate a holistic human being who can think critically, empathize deeply, and act purposefully.

By aligning these elements, Achyuta Samanta's holistic vision ensures that education addresses not only academic and practical needs but also emotional and ethical dimensions, creating empowered, capable, and compassionate global citizens.

Educational Practices at KISS

At **Kalinga Institute of Social Sciences (KISS)**, Prof. Samanta has turned his vision of all-round development into a vibrant reality. The institution's unique approach ensures that every student receives a well-rounded education that caters to all aspects of their personality.

1. **Physical Development**:

Physical fitness is given prime importance, with regular sports, yoga, and outdoor activities integrated into the curriculum. These activities are designed to promote a healthy lifestyle, build teamwork, and develop resilience.

2. **Mental and Emotional Growth**:

Intellectual growth is fostered through a rigorous academic curriculum that includes critical thinking, innovation, and problem-solving. In addition, emotional intelligence is nurtured through cultural and extracurricular activities that promote empathy, teamwork, and self-awareness.

3. **Spiritual and Moral Development**:

Students are encouraged to explore their inner selves through meditation, reflection, and discussions on ethics and values. This spiritual growth helps them develop a sense of inner peace and moral responsibility, which is essential for becoming compassionate individuals who contribute positively to society.

4. **Vocational and Practical Skills**: KISS places a strong emphasis on practical skills by offering a variety of vocational training programs such as **handicrafts, agriculture, technology, and entrepreneurship**. This enables students to gain the necessary skills for self-sufficiency and empowers them to lead productive lives, contributing to their communities.

5. **Aesthetic and Social Development**: Cultural and artistic activities such as music, dance, drama, and arts are deeply embedded in the educational journey at KISS. These activities promote creativity, aesthetic appreciation, and social cohesion, helping students express themselves and develop a sense of belonging.

Core Philosophy

1. **Holistic Development**: True education aims at developing all aspects of the child—intellectual, physical, emotional, social, moral, and spiritual—in harmony.

2. **Education for Life**: Learning should not be confined to academic subjects alone but should extend to life skills, emotional intelligence, and personal growth.

3. **Balance of Head, Heart, and Hand**: Intellectual, emotional, and practical development should work in tandem to foster well-rounded, responsible, and skilled individuals.

4. **Education for Empowerment**: By developing vocational and life skills, education empowers individuals to lead self-reliant and meaningful lives.

Inspirational Tagline
"Head, Heart, and Hand—educating for the mind, soul, and future."
Prof. Achyuta Samanta's philosophy of **all-round development** goes beyond traditional education. It nurtures the entire child, ensuring that they grow into compassionate, skilled, and responsible individuals who can contribute meaningfully to society. At KISS, this vision is brought to life, where students are educated not only in academics but also in life skills, values, and culture.

In Prof. Samanta's words:
"True education does not only cultivate knowledge; it nurtures the soul, trains the hands, and develops the heart. It is through the balanced growth of all aspects of a child's personality that we prepare them to meet the world with confidence, compassion, and competence."

This holistic approach has made KISS a model institution, where students are empowered to excel academically, live meaningfully, and serve their communities with love and dedication.

6. Spiritual Development
In the land of India, where spirituality is deeply embedded in its culture and traditions, Prof. Achyuta Samanta believes that **spiritual enlightenment** is not just an optional pursuit but a vital necessity for living in peace and harmony. He emphasizes the importance of nurturing the **spiritual dimension** of a child's growth, recognizing that, in today's world, where materialism often dominates, a deeper connection with the soul is essential for fostering true peace and understanding.

Spiritual Practices at KISS
At KISS, Prof. Samanta's commitment to spiritual development is evident in the daily practices and celebrations that are integrated into the curriculum. These spiritual observances not only foster cultural pride but also provide students with opportunities to experience and internalize the values of peace, devotion, and respect for all living beings.

Some of the key practices include:
1. **Festivals and Observances**:
   - **Ganesh Puja**, **Saraswati Puja**, and the **Chariot Festival** are celebrated with great enthusiasm within the KISS

campus. These spiritual events help students connect with their cultural roots and engage in practices that promote inner reflection, humility, and gratitude.

- These festivals also serve as a reminder of the importance of worship and reverence for higher values, offering students opportunities to seek blessings for wisdom, knowledge, and success.

2. **Spiritual Guidance in Education**:
   - Prof. Samanta advises that teachers in KISS should incorporate **spiritual principles** into their teaching methods. This means guiding students to not just excel academically but also to grow in moral and spiritual wisdom. Teachers are encouraged to model values such as kindness, respect, and compassion, creating an atmosphere where students feel safe and nurtured spiritually.

3. **KISS (Sankha) Srivani kshetra:**

   One of the most remarkable examples of **Prof. Samanta's vision** is the creation of the **KISS (Sankha) Srivani Kshyatra**, a sacred space designed to offer students a chance to experience spiritual growth through **rituals**, **worship**, and **meditation**. The Sankha Kshyatra is a

replica of Puri, Odisha's revered spiritual center, and serves as a **living embodiment of India's spiritual heritage**. It features multiple sacred spaces, each dedicated to fostering spiritual practices and teachings:

- **Shiva Temple**: A place for students to seek blessings and practice devotion through prayer and meditation, fostering a connection to Lord Shiva, the symbol of transformation and liberation.
- **Maa Lakshmi Temple**: Dedicated to **Maa Lakshmi**, the goddess of wealth and prosperity, this temple serves as a place for students to reflect on the importance of abundance—not just material, but also in terms of wisdom, love, and spiritual growth.
- **Maa Bhubaneswari Temple**: A space dedicated to the **Mother Goddess**, Maa Bhubaneswari, known for her strength and compassion, offering students an opportunity to connect with the nurturing and protective aspects of spirituality.
- **Ganesh Temple**: A center dedicated to **Lord Ganesha**, the remover of obstacles, helping students overcome the challenges they face in their academic and personal lives.
- **Maa Lakshmi's Kitchen (Avada Arna Making)**: A special space within the Kshyatra where students can engage in making **Avada Arna** (Maa Lakshmi's offerings), teaching them the values of **service**, **humility**, and **self-sufficiency** through hands-on activities that also promote a sense of unity and shared purpose.
- **Hawan Kunda**: An area for students and faculty to perform **Hawan** (sacred fire rituals), which is believed to purify the mind, body, and environment, and bring peace and prosperity to all who participate.

Profound Quote and Reflection

In the words of **Professor Rusk**, "Education must enable mankind through its culture to enter more and more fully into the spiritual realm and also enlarge the boundaries of the spiritual realm." Prof. Samanta believes that education should act as a **gateway to spirituality**, expanding the boundaries of the mind and spirit, guiding individuals to a higher level of consciousness and self-realization.

At KISS, this philosophy comes alive in the daily practices, the celebrations, and the spaces like **Sankha Kshyatra**, where students are not only educated in subjects but also spiritually nurtured to become compassionate, enlightened human beings who can positively contribute to society.

Heart-Touching Reflection

Prof. Samanta's approach to **spiritual development** goes beyond traditional education. It calls on every individual to **connect with their inner self** and to recognize the divine essence within every person. In today's fast-paced and often materialistic world, this kind of spiritual grounding is more important than ever.

Through initiatives like **KISS Sankha Kshyatra** and the institution's emphasis on daily spiritual observances, KISS not only educates students but also transforms them—imbuing them with a sense of **peace, purpose, and interconnectedness** with the world around them.

It is through this profound integration of **spirituality in education** that Prof. Samanta's vision for **holistic development** becomes a reality, creating a generation of leaders who are not only academically successful but also spiritually awakened, morally grounded, and compassionately engaged in the world.

Core Philosophy

Prof. Samanta's belief is rooted in the idea that education must not only develop the **mind and body** but also **the spirit**. He understands that it is only through spiritual growth that individuals can cultivate inner peace, emotional intelligence, and a sense of unity with the world. Thus, he places greater importance on **spiritual values** than material wealth or success, knowing that material attainments often fade, but the development of the spirit endures forever.

He further emphasizes that the **goal of education** is to guide the child to develop **mentally, morally, and spiritually**, ensuring that they grow into well-rounded individuals capable of contributing meaningfully to society. This emphasis on spiritual growth is an essential aspect of **Prof. Samanta's educational philosophy** and the atmosphere of **Kalinga Institute of Social Sciences (KISS)**.

Inspirational Tagline of him

"Spiritual growth is the foundation of true education—a journey of self-discovery and universal connection."

In his words:

"Education that touches only the mind is incomplete. True education must awaken the spirit within, nurturing kindness, humility, and inner peace. When a child learns to find strength in prayer, compassion in action, and unity in all beings, only then has education truly fulfilled its purpose."

7. Development of Inventive and Creative Power

Prof. Samanta's educational philosophy places great emphasis on the **development of inventive and creative powers**, especially for those who have historically been marginalized, such as the **tribal communities**. For Prof. Samanta, the transformative power of **education** lies in its ability to ignite the creative and inventive capacities of every child, enabling them to not only adapt to the changing world but to also shape and influence it in meaningful ways.

His belief is simple but profound: **education** is the key that unlocks the potential for individuals to transform their **environment** and **society**, making it more aligned with their needs and aspirations. For **tribal students**, education becomes a **tool of empowerment**, offering them a platform where their inherent creative talents can flourish and where they can actively contribute to the shaping of their own futures.

Practical Implementation at KISS

At **KISS**, Prof. Samanta's commitment to the development of **inventive and creative power** is clearly seen through the diverse **activities** and **programs** designed to foster creativity and practical skills in students. These initiatives aim to empower students to not only excel academically but also to develop **hands-on skills** that can help them **change** and **improve** their environments.

1. **Art and Craft Programs:**
   - Students are encouraged to engage in various forms of **art** and **craft**, which helps them express their creativity, understand the world around them, and find innovative ways to utilize resources. These programs enable students to explore their **artistic talents** while also giving them the **skills** to create **functional** and **aesthetic** pieces that are useful in everyday life.

2. **Vocational Education:**
   - Vocational training is a key aspect of the **curriculum at KISS**, designed to equip students with **practical skills** that are directly applicable in the real world. Prof. Samanta emphasizes that education must go beyond traditional classroom learning and must include **hands-on, skill-based training** that prepares students for the **vocational challenges** they may

face in their communities and the world at large. Programs like **candle making, phenyl production, toys making**, and more not only enhance creativity but also provide students with the **tools** to become **self-reliant**.

3. **Games and Sports**:
   - **Sports** and **physical activities** are integrated into the educational framework as a means of **stimulating creativity** and **problem-solving skills**. By participating in **team sports** and **individual games**, students develop the ability to think **strategically**, enhance their **physical well-being**, and learn the value of **teamwork** and **resilience**. These activities foster creativity by encouraging students to think on their feet and adapt quickly to challenges.

4. **Independent Projects and Exploration**:
   - Prof. Samanta believes that giving students the **freedom** to explore and experiment is essential in fostering their **inventive powers**. At KISS, students are encouraged to work on **independent projects**, where they can apply their knowledge and creativity to solve real-world problems. This process not only develops their inventive abilities but also gives them a sense of ownership over their learning and their **future success**.

Heart-Touching Reflection

At **KISS**, the development of **inventive and creative power** is more than just a goal; it is a **mission** that **empowers** each student to become an agent of **change**. Prof. Samanta's vision is clear: **education should liberate the potential within every child**, allowing them to not only survive but to thrive and transform their communities through **creativity**, **innovation**, and **independent thinking**.

Through his efforts, **tribal students**, often overlooked by mainstream education, are provided with the tools and opportunities to shape not just their own lives but also the world around them. The **projects, vocational programs**, and **creative initiatives** at KISS are a testament to the belief that every child has the ability to contribute creatively to society, given the right environment and guidance.

Core Philosophy

Prof. Samanta's philosophy centers on **fostering creativity** and **innovation** through education, providing children the **freedom to explore** and develop their **innate talents**. His vision is not merely to impart knowledge but to cultivate **independent thinking** and a **sense of agency**, empowering students to **shape their own destinies** through creative expression and invention. This vision is deeply rooted in the belief that **education should provide the tools to modify and adapt the physical environment** to meet human needs, ensuring that students develop the **skills to master materials** and resources in innovative ways.

Inspirational Tagline of him

"Through education, we shape the future—empowering every child to create, invent, and change the world."

In his words:

"Creativity is the heartbeat of progress. When a child is given the freedom to dream, explore, and build, education becomes a tool not just for learning, but for transforming lives and communities. True empowerment begins when imagination is nurtured into invention."

8. Aesthetic Development

Aesthetic development, in Prof. Samanta's educational philosophy, refers to the cultivation of **appreciation for beauty** and an **understanding of the criteria for judging beauty**. It involves the awakening of **sensory awareness** and a deep connection to the beautiful experiences that surround us. For Prof. Samanta, the essence of **aesthetic development** is not just in recognizing beauty but in **engaging with it** in a way that fosters creativity, joy, and positivity.

He strongly believed that **children** inherently possess **creative potential** and a natural inclination towards beauty. However, in the present day, many educators fail to nurture and encourage this sense of **aesthetic appreciation** in students. Prof. Samanta sought to change this by fostering an environment where **aesthetic sensibilities** are actively cultivated, allowing students to appreciate and create beauty around them.

Practical Implementation at KISS

At **KISS**, Prof. Samanta's commitment to **aesthetic development** is vividly manifested through several initiatives aimed at nurturing students' creative expression and appreciation for beauty. His approach to creating a **beautiful learning environment** emphasizes **participation, engagement,** and **creativity**, allowing students to express their own aesthetic sensibilities while **enhancing** the overall atmosphere of the institution.

1. **Arts and Crafts Gallery**:
   - Prof. Samanta introduced a **dedicated Arts and Crafts Gallery** at KISS, where students are encouraged to showcase their **creative works**. This gallery serves as a space for students to express their **artistic talents** and  engage in **artistic exploration**, allowing them to develop their **aesthetic sensibilities** and share their creativity with the wider community. This initiative nurtures both **individual creativity** and **collective appreciation** for art within the campus.

2. **Campus Beautification Program**:
   - The **Campus Beautification Program** at KISS is an initiative that encourages every student to participate in **gardening** and **plantation**, fostering a love for nature and the beauty of 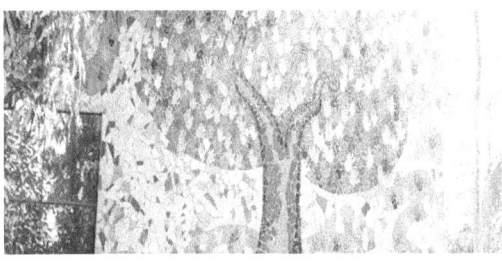 the environment. Students contribute to the **design** and **maintenance** of the **campus landscape**, ensuring that it is both aesthetically pleasing and environmentally friendly. The vibrant flowers and plants throughout the year not only beautify the surroundings but also create a peaceful and positive atmosphere conducive to learning.

3. **Postcard and Calendar Reproductions**:
   - To inspire students further, Prof. Samanta introduced the idea of creating **postcard**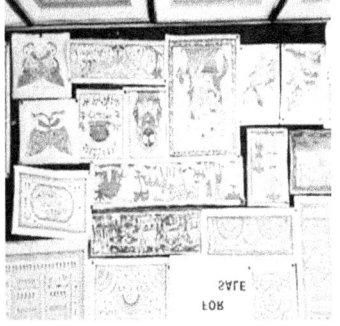

and **calendar reproductions** of **artwork** from local **artists**, as well as notable pieces of **cultural significance**. These artworks are displayed in the **museum**, **hostels**, and **corridors** of the institution, transforming the campus into an **art gallery** that immerses students in beauty as they go about their daily routines. The vibrant display of art throughout the campus nurtures students' aesthetic growth by constantly exposing them to new forms of creativity.

4. **Field Trips and Educational Tours**:
   - To broaden students' exposure to beauty, KISS organizes **field trips** and **educational tours** to some of the most iconic and aesthetically rich locations in India. These include places like **Konark** and **Puri**, where students can witness the **architecture, sculptures**, and **art** that have defined Indian heritage for centuries. These trips serve as immersive experiences that **inspire creativity** and deepen students' understanding of cultural and aesthetic values.

5. **Seminars with Local Artists**:
   - Prof. Samanta also initiated **seminars with local artists** where they are invited to share their time, ideas, and work with students. This initiative fosters **collaboration** between students and experienced artists, providing them with valuable **insights** into the world of **art** and **aesthetic creation**. These seminars help students connect with the **local artistic community** and gain **hands-on experiences** that enhance their own artistic expression.

KISS exemplifies Prof. Samanta's vision of a **holistic environment** where **aesthetic development** is woven into every aspect of the institution. The campus itself is a **testament to beauty** and **creativity**, with its **floras** and **faunas** enhancing the serene and positive atmosphere. The entire institution is filled with **flowers, statues of great men**, and other aesthetic elements that inspire both students and staff to appreciate beauty in its many forms. The **sculptures** and **idols of great men** placed throughout the campus serve as reminders of the **importance of creativity** and the **spiritual connection to beauty**.

This environment encourages students to **experience beauty** not only in **art** but also in **nature** and **culture**, helping them to develop a deeper sense of **aesthetic appreciation**. Whether it's the gardens, the murals, or the statues, the entire campus acts as an **artistic space**, designed to foster a sense of **peace, joy**, and **creativity** in the hearts of every student.

Heart-Touching Reflection

Prof. Samanta's dedication to **aesthetic development** at KISS is a profound expression of his belief that **education** is not just about the **mind** but also about cultivating a **spirit of beauty** that nourishes the **soul**. By nurturing students' creativity and helping them **appreciate beauty**, Prof. Samanta is instilling in them the values of **peace, positivity**, and **joy** that will stay with them throughout their lives.

As he always emphasizes to his teachers, education should teach children to **cherish beauty** in everything they experience. Whether in nature, in art, or in the people around them, beauty can be a **source of inspiration** and **positivity**—a true reflection of the **holistic** approach to education that Prof. Samanta has so passionately implemented.

Core Philosophy

Prof. Samanta's belief is that **aesthetic development** is not just about creating beautiful things, but about fostering a **deeper emotional connection** to the world around us. He believed that **art** and **beauty** have the power to uplift the human spirit, spark creativity, and provide a sense of **positivity** and **inspiration**. Therefore, his educational philosophy integrates **aesthetic development** as an essential component of **holistic education**—one that nurtures the body, mind, and soul.

He emphasized that **educators** should not only guide students in **academic pursuits**, but also help them develop an appreciation for **beauty** in **art, nature**, and **life**. His ultimate aim was to help children **cherish beauty** and find **joy** in experiencing the **aesthetic qualities** of the world around them.

Inspirational Tagline

"Let education nurture not only the mind, but also the soul, by fostering a lifelong love for beauty and creativity."

In his words:

"Beauty uplifts the soul. When children learn to see and create beauty—in art, in nature, and in life they carry within them a wellspring of joy, peace, and creativity that no hardship can erase."

9. Vocational Self-Reliance: Building a Sustainable Future

In the modern world, earning a livelihood has become increasingly challenging. Recognizing this societal need, **Prof. Samanta Sir** has emphasized that the aim of education should be oriented toward **vocational self-reliance**. He believes education must empower individuals to support themselves and contribute meaningfully to society, ensuring they are not dependent on others for even their basic necessities.

Prof. Samanta stresses that education should be **utilitarian** rather than ornamental. In his view, if education does not equip individuals to stand on their own feet, it loses its significance. An individual who becomes a **parasite** on society fails to meet the true purpose of education. To address this, Prof. Samanta integrates **vocational education** as a critical component of learning, enabling students to earn a livelihood with dignity and pride.

Practical Implementation at KISS

At **KISS**, this philosophy is brought to life through a diverse array of **vocational training programs**. These initiatives not only address the **bread and butter** needs of education but also foster a sense of **purpose** and **self-worth** among students.

1. **Extensive Vocational Training Programs**:

Prof. Samanta has introduced a wide range of **vocational courses** that cater to the diverse interests and aptitudes of students. These programs include:

- **Tailoring** and **Appliqué Work**: Students are taught traditional and modern tailoring skills, which can lead to sustainable livelihoods.
- **Soft Toy Making**: Encouraging creativity and entrepreneurship.
- **Chemical Production**: Training in making phenyl, hand wash, dish wash, and other chemical products for household and commercial use.
- **Food Processing**: Teaching students to make pickles, spices, and processed foods to cater to growing demands.

- **Animal Husbandry**: Aimed at students from rural backgrounds to enhance their skills in dairy farming, poultry, and livestock care.
- **Painting and Art**: Providing creative outlets with potential for commercial success.
- **Medical Attendant Training**: Preparing students for careers in healthcare.
- **Mineral Water Production**: Developing skills in water purification and bottling.

2. **Integration with Holistic Education**:

These vocational courses are seamlessly integrated into the academic curriculum, ensuring that students graduate not only with knowledge but also with practical skills. This dual approach enhances their employability and prepares them for the challenges of a competitive world.

3. **Skill-Based Learning Centers**:

Dedicated centers for vocational training have been established within the **KISS** campus. These centers provide students with hands-on experience and expert guidance, enabling them to master their chosen crafts.

4. **Entrepreneurship Development**:

Prof. Samanta also promotes entrepreneurial thinking among students. By learning vocational skills, students are encouraged to start their own businesses, creating job opportunities for themselves and others.

5. **Real-World Exposure**:

Students participate in internships and collaborations with **government** and **non-government organizations**, providing them with exposure to real-world challenges and opportunities.

A Heart-Touching Example

The impact of vocational education at KISS is best illustrated by the transformation of its students. Many tribal students, who once struggled to envision a future beyond subsistence farming, are now running **small-scale enterprises** or contributing to industries as skilled workers. For example, a group of students trained in food processing now runs a successful business producing organic pickles, while others have turned their tailoring skills into thriving garment shops in their communities.

These success stories reflect the **self-reliance** that Prof. Samanta envisioned, proving that education can be a tool for **economic empowerment** and **social transformation**.

Core Philosophy

At the heart of this initiative is Prof. Samanta's belief in fostering **self-reliance** among students. His philosophy aligns with the idea that education should not only nurture intellectual growth but also instill practical skills that prepare individuals for **real-world challenges**. By equipping students with vocational expertise, he ensures they are **economically empowered**, independent, and able to contribute to society effectively.

Prof. Samanta's philosophy emphasizes that vocational education is not just about earning a living; it is about **dignity of labor, self-confidence**, and **economic freedom**. It is a pathway to personal growth and societal progress, particularly for underserved communities.

Inspirational Tagline of him

"From Learning to Earning: Vocational Education at KISS Builds a Self-Reliant Future."

In his words:
"True education teaches a child to stand on their own feet. When learning leads to earning, dignity follows—and with it, a life of self-respect and purpose."

10. Education for Employability and Life Skills

Prof. Samanta Sir believes that education should not only nurture intellectual development but also empower students with **employability and life skills**. For him, the best learning happens when it is **connected, interactive, practical, and enjoyable**, offering students the freedom to make choices about their learning journey. He emphasizes that education for employability ensures that students develop the **personal qualities, practical skills, broader knowledge base, and attitudes** necessary for lifelong learning and work in an ever-changing world.

By connecting education to employability, Prof. Samanta ensures that the learning process becomes **relevant and transformative**, enabling students to connect what they learn with their lives and actively participate in shaping their future.

Vocational Programs and Partnerships at KISS

The employability programs at **KISS** are meticulously designed to cater to students from diverse socioeconomic backgrounds, particularly those from underprivileged sections. Below are some of the ongoing initiatives:
1. **IL&FS (Infrastructure Leasing & Financial Services):**

- Short-term placement-linked training programs conducted by an NGO under the following trades:
    - Sewing Machine Operator
    - Customer Care Executive for Call Centers
    - General Duty Attendant
    - X-Ray Technician (for science students)
    - Electrician
    - AC Refrigeration Technician

    This program addresses the needs of students from financially weaker backgrounds or those with less interest in general education. It ensures **immediate employment** after training in companies and organizations, providing a pathway to financial stability.

2. **PMKVY (Pradhan Mantri Kaushal Vikas Yojana):**
    - A flagship central government program offering vocational training in trades such as:
        - Assistant Electrician
        - Customer Care Executive
        - Field Technician AC
        - Plumber Technician
        - General Data Entry Operator
        - Welding Technician
        - Retail Services
        - BFSI (Banking, Financial Services, and Insurance)

    This initiative empowers students with skills that make them employable in government and private sectors. It also includes **loan facilities** to help trained students establish small-scale industries.

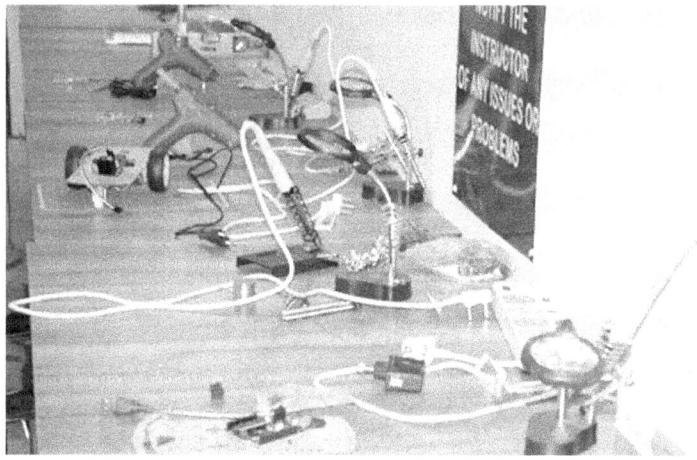

3. **TCS (Tata Consultancy Services):**
   - A three-to-four-month training program led by TCS experts, which includes:
     - Office Maintenance
     - Data Entry Operations
     - Managerial Services

   Students are provided **on-campus training**, followed by a written exam and an interview. Successful candidates are offered positions in TCS, reflecting a seamless transition from learning to employment.

4. **SDT/PLET (Skill Development Training/Placement Linked Employment Program):**
   - A government of Odisha initiative targeting slow learners or those with an interest in industrial training. Trades offered include:
     - Fitter
     - Welder
     - Assistant Electrician
     - Sewing Machine Operator

   Participants receive a certification upon completion, equipping them with industry-ready skills and access to employment in high-demand industrial sectors.

5. **Schneider Electrical Program:**
   - Conducted in collaboration with Schneider Electrical Company, this program focuses on training students in:
     - Electrical Equipment Repairing
     - House Electrical Wiring

   The company invested over **7 lakh** to establish an electrical training center on campus, ensuring students gain practical, hands-on skills that provide **sustainable livelihoods** after graduation.

Recent Employability Opportunities at KISS

In response to evolving industry demands, KISS has introduced **new vocational courses and partnerships**. These recent developments enhance its already robust employability framework:

1. **AI & Digital Skills Program** (New):
   - In collaboration with a leading tech company, KISS now offers specialized training in:
     - Basic and Advanced Computer Skills
     - Artificial Intelligence and Machine Learning Basics

- Digital Marketing and E-Commerce Operations

Students completing this program are offered internships and placement opportunities with tech startups and established firms.

2. **Healthcare Vocational Training Expansion** (New):
   - Building on its existing programs, KISS has partnered with a reputed hospital chain to provide training in:
     - Phlebotomy (Blood Sample Collection)
     - Medical Laboratory Assistance
     - Geriatric Care and Home Nursing

   These new streams address the growing demand in the healthcare sector, ensuring students can access job opportunities across hospitals, diagnostic labs, and eldercare facilities.

3. **Green Technology & Sustainability Skills** (New):
   - Recognizing the importance of sustainable development, KISS has launched programs in collaboration with environmental organizations, offering training in:

     - Solar Panel Installation and Maintenance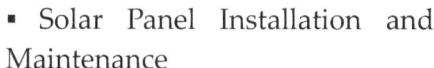

     - Organic Farming and Agro-Processing
     - Waste Management and Recycling

     These courses equip students with skills that not only create job opportunities but also contribute to community and environmental well-being.

4. **Hospitality and Tourism Management Program:**
   - With Odisha being a hub for tourism, KISS has introduced additional training in:
     - Hotel Operations and Management
     - Front Desk and Guest Relations
     - Food and Beverage Services

   Students trained in this program are offered employment in renowned hotels, resorts, and travel agencies across India.

5. **Entrepreneurship and Start-up Incubation** (New):
   - To nurture entrepreneurial spirit, KISS has set up a **Start-up Incubation Cell**, providing:

- Business Idea Workshops
- Financial Management Training
- Access to Seed Funding through government and private initiatives

This initiative supports students who wish to start their own ventures, with mentorship from industry experts.

Life Skills beyond Employment
Life Skills Training at KISS

Prof. Samanta Sir emphasizes life skills education as an integral part of holistic development at KISS, fostering resilience, adaptability, and confidence in students to navigate life's challenges. In collaboration with the **United Nations Population Fund (UNFPA)**, KISS has implemented an impactful **Life Skills Education Program**, tailored to the needs of tribal students. The program integrates theoretical knowledge with practical applications to empower students with essential skills for personal, social, and professional success.

1. **Self-Awareness**
- **Definition**: Understanding oneself, including strengths, weaknesses, emotions, and values.
- **Activities**:
   - **Self-Reflection Workshops**: Students participate in group exercises to identify their strengths and aspirations.
   - **Journaling Sessions**: Encourages daily introspection and tracking emotional patterns.
- **Example**: Students reflect on their career goals during UNFPA-led workshops, which guide them to choose suitable vocational training programs.

2. **Empathy**
- **Definition**: The ability to understand and share the feelings of others.
- **Activities**:
   - **Role-Playing Exercises**: Helps students understand diverse perspectives, especially during cultural or social awareness sessions.
   - **Community Outreach Programs**: Students visit nearby villages to teach children or assist elders.
- **Example**: During the "Peer Educators Program" by UNFPA, senior students help juniors understand sensitive issues like gender equality and reproductive health.

3. **Effective Communication**
- **Definition**: Expressing ideas and emotions clearly and confidently, both verbally and non-verbally.
- **Activities**:
  - **Debate and Speech Competitions**: Focused on current social issues like climate change and gender equality.
  - **Workshops by Resource Persons**: Training in body language and public speaking.
- **Example**: In a UNFPA-led session on "Gender Roles," students practice articulating their opinions on breaking stereotypes.

4. **Critical Thinking**
- **Definition**: The ability to analyze information and evaluate arguments logically.
- **Activities**:
  - **Problem-Solving Challenges**: Students work on real-life scenarios, such as planning a community event.
  - **Debates on Ethical Dilemmas**: Guided by external trainers from organizations like UNFPA.
- **Example**: A student group brainstorms ways to improve sanitation in their village, presenting ideas to local authorities.

5. **Decision-Making**
- **Definition**: Choosing the best course of action after evaluating different options.
- **Activities**:
  - **Simulation Games**: Encouraging students to solve hypothetical life challenges, such as budgeting for family needs.
  - **Career Guidance Sessions**: Students evaluate options with mentors before finalizing a vocational or academic path.
- **Example**: UNFPA organizes a career decision-making workshop where students map their interests to various professions.

6. **Problem-Solving**
- **Definition**: The ability to find constructive solutions to issues.
- **Activities**:
  - **Real-Life Problem Simulations**: Examples include addressing bullying or managing group conflicts.
  - **DIY (Do-It-Yourself) Projects**: Students create solutions for common problems, like making eco-friendly products.
- **Example**: A group project focuses on creating affordable hand wash solutions during hygiene campaigns.

7. **Interpersonal Relationships**
- **Definition**: Building and maintaining healthy, meaningful relationships.
- **Activities**:
  - **Team Sports and Group Activities**: Focused on collaboration and camaraderie.
  - **Peer Mentorship Programs**: Seniors guide juniors on academic and personal challenges.
- **Example**: Students build strong peer bonds while organizing cultural programs like Saraswati Puja or community service events.

8. **Coping with Stress**
- **Definition**: Managing stress positively through resilience-building practices.
- **Activities**:
  - **Meditation and Yoga Classes**: Regularly conducted by experts to improve mental health.
  - **Stress Management Workshops**: Organized by UNFPA and local mental health organizations.
- **Example**: During exams, workshops teach relaxation techniques like deep breathing to reduce anxiety.

9. **Coping with Emotions**
- **Definition**: Recognizing and managing one's emotions constructively.
- **Activities**:
  - **Drama and Role-Play**: Students enact scenarios to understand emotional triggers and responses.
  - **Art Therapy Sessions**: Facilitated by local artists to help students express emotions creatively.
- **Example**: Students draw and discuss their emotions during workshops on emotional well-being.

10. **Creative Thinking**
- **Definition**: The ability to think outside the box and generate innovative ideas.
- **Activities**:
  - **Creative Art and Craft Workshops**: Students design models, toys, or other crafts.
  - **Innovation Challenges**: Projects like creating eco-friendly products or improving campus facilities.
- **Example**: In an art session, students design posters for a health awareness campaign, showcasing their creativity.

Collaborations and Expert Guidance
The implementation of these life skills is enriched by collaborations with various organizations, including:
- **UNFPA**: Conducts workshops on gender sensitivity, reproductive health, and self-awareness.
- **TCS and IL&FS**: Provide employability skills training, integrating decision-making and problem-solving in workplace contexts.
- **Local NGOs and Resource Persons**: Facilitate art therapy, meditation, and practical life skills training.

Examples of Activities Organized Yearly
1. **Life Skills Week**:
    - Students participate in a series of workshops, sports, and interactive sessions, focusing on all 10 life skills.

2. **Educational Tours**:
    - Visits to cultural sites like Konark or Puri teach critical thinking and interpersonal skills.
3. **Community Engagement Days**:
    - Activities like tree planting and village clean-up projects combine empathy, teamwork, and problem-solving.

Life Skills in Action: Holistic Learning at KISS
By integrating these life skills into everyday education, KISS ensures students not only excel academically but also grow into capable, compassionate, and resilient individuals, ready to face the challenges of life.

Core Philosophy
At the heart of this initiative is the idea that **education is the greatest enabler of self-reliance**. Prof. Samanta believes in equipping students, especially those from marginalized communities, with the skills and opportunities required to become contributors to society. His vision for employability extends beyond mere job placement—it is about building **confidence, independence, and a sense of purpose**.

To meet these objectives, he has forged partnerships and signed **Memorandums of Understanding (MOUs)** with leading government and private organizations. These partnerships provide students with practical training, industry exposure, and direct employment opportunities, bringing his philosophy of holistic and vocational education to life.

Inspirational Tagline of him

"From Education to Employment: Empowering Lives, Building Futures at KISS."

"Empowering Minds, Enriching Lives: Life Skills for a Sustainable Future."

In His Words:

"True education teaches a child to stand on their own feet. When learning leads to earning, dignity follows—and with it, a life of self-respect and purpose. At KISS, we link learning with life by offering practical skills, vocational training, and life skills education that empower every child to live with confidence, independence, and compassion."

The recent additions to KISS's employability initiatives have opened doors to cutting-edge careers, ensuring students are equipped to meet the demands of the modern workforce. Many graduates now excel in fields like **technology, healthcare, tourism, and green technology**, with others successfully launching their own enterprises.

11. Preservation and Transmission of Culture

Prof. Achyuta Samanta firmly believes that education must serve as a medium to preserve and transmit culture, as culture defines identity and reflects the essence of a community. He acknowledges that India is globally renowned for its rich and diverse cultural heritage, and this legacy must be passed down to future generations. According to him, the aim of education is to nurture this heritage while fostering the intellect, intelligence, and creativity needed to enrich it further.

At KISS, this philosophy is deeply integrated, as the institution is home to thousands of **Adivasi students**, each with unique cultural traditions and practices. For these students, culture is not merely an aspect of life but an intrinsic part of their identity. Prof. Samanta Sir emphasizes the importance of education in helping students preserve their cultural roots while equipping them with the skills and confidence to share these traditions with the world.

Key Initiatives to Preserve and Transmit Culture at KISS
1. Celebration of Tribal Festivals and Rituals
- Festivals such as **Sarad Utsav**, **Baha Parab**, **Karam Parab**, **Chaitra Parab**, and **Makar Sankranti** are celebrated with student-led performances showcasing traditional rituals, songs, and dances like *Ghumura*, *Dhemsa*, and *Sambalpuri*.

- **Sacred Practices**: The institution organizes cultural rituals specific to various tribes, allowing students to participate and learn their significance.

He believes *"Festivals are the living classrooms of heritage."*

2. *Integration of Tribal Art and Craft into Education*
- **Arts and Crafts Workshops**: KISS collaborates with local and national artists to teach students traditional crafts such as tribal painting, pottery, and weaving.

- The **KISS Art Gallery** displays students' work, showcasing their creativity and preserving tribal art forms.

Example Activity: Workshops on tribal wall painting (*Sohrai* and *Saura art*), clay modeling, and bamboo craft.

He believes "Creativity blossoms where culture breathes."

3. *Promotion of Tribal Languages*
- **Language Classes**: Tribal languages such as Santali, Kui, and Ho are taught through dedicated programs, ensuring their preservation.
- **Storytelling and Oral Traditions**: Students document and share folklore, myths, and traditional tales in their native languages.

He believes "Language is the soul of culture."

4. *Cultural Exchange and Global Recognition*
- **Performances at International Forums**: KISS students represent tribal cultures on global platforms, including **UNICEF's Global Tribal Festival** and UNESCO events.
- **Exchange Programs**: Collaboration with schools and universities globally fosters respect and understanding of diverse cultures.

He believes "From tribal roots to global heights."

5. *Heritage Documentation and Research*
- Students are encouraged to document the history, rituals, and cultural practices of their communities as part of research projects.
- **Heritage Repository**: A digital archive is being developed to preserve tribal knowledge for future generations.

He believes "Knowledge preserved is culture enriched."

Enhancing Campus Culture Through Aesthetic Integration
- **Campus Beautification Program:** Inspired by tribal aesthetics, students participate in creating murals, planting gardens, and designing spaces.
- **Cultural Displays:** Statues of tribal leaders, historical figures, and artwork reflecting tribal life are strategically placed across the campus to inspire pride and curiosity.

He believes "A beautiful campus mirrors a rich culture."

Cultural Awareness as Holistic Development

At KISS, cultural education aligns seamlessly with Prof. Samanta's holistic educational philosophy. Activities focus on fostering:

- **Identity and Pride:** Students learn to cherish their cultural roots while thriving in the modern world.
- **Moral and Ethical Values:** Derived from traditional practices and stories.
- **Aesthetic Sensibility and Creativity:** Through arts, crafts, and beautification projects.

He believes "Culture shapes character; education amplifies it."

Core Philosophy

Prof. Achyuta Samanta believes that education serves as a bridge between the past, present, and future, ensuring that cultural identity and heritage are preserved and transmitted across generations. He emphasizes that cultural education must go beyond textbooks to instill pride, understanding, and respect for traditions while preparing individuals to adapt these values to modern realities.

KISS exemplifies this philosophy through its efforts to preserve and celebrate the rich and diverse cultural heritage of India, particularly focusing on the unique tribal traditions of its students. The institution integrates cultural preservation as a core component of holistic education, fostering respect for diversity and global recognition of India's indigenous cultures.

Inspirational Tagline of him

"Education must preserve the roots of identity and transmit the richness of our heritage to illuminate the future."

In His Words:

"Education must preserve the roots of identity and transmit the richness of our heritage to illuminate the future. Culture is not a subject—it is the soul of who we are. At KISS, every festival, language, and tradition is a lesson in pride, unity, and timeless wisdom." — Prof. Achyuta Samanta

12. Empowerment of Women

Through its innovative strategies, KISS has proven that empowering women through education can transform entire communities. By nurturing tribal girls into confident, skilled, and self-reliant individuals, Prof. Samanta's vision of holistic education is realized.

"Empowering women is not just a mission; it is a movement toward a better and equitable world," says Prof. Samanta. Under his leadership, KISS is a beacon of hope and a global model for women's empowerment through education.

Key Initiatives to empower women at KISS
Breaking Barriers Through Education

Prof. Samanta identified the root challenges in tribal areas that hinder girls' education:

1. **Poor Enrolment and Retention:** Cultural practices and economic conditions compel girls to focus on household chores and sibling care.
2. **Distance from Schools:** Geographic isolation leads to high dropout rates among tribal girls.
3. **Societal Attitudes:** Traditional norms often restrict girls' access to education and mobility.

To address these issues, he adopted a gender-sensitive approach:

- KISS ensures a **60:40 admission ratio of girls to boys**, giving priority to girls.
- **Residential Education:** By providing a safe, inclusive, and accessible campus environment, KISS removes barriers like distance and domestic workload.

Health, Hygiene, and Life Skills Education

Recognizing that education for empowerment must address physical and emotional well-being, KISS focuses on:

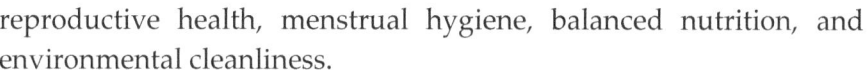

1. *Adolescent Reproductive and Sexual Health (ARSH):*
   - **Dedicated Classes:** ARSH sessions are mandatory for all girl students, where they learn about reproductive health, menstrual hygiene, balanced nutrition, and environmental cleanliness.
   - **Girl-Friendly Facilities:** Separate toilets with amenities tailored for girls' needs, such as sanitary pads and proper drainage, are maintained with community participation.
   - **Personal Hygiene Awareness Campaigns:** Regular workshops are conducted in collaboration with organizations like **UNFPA** to address taboo topics and promote confidence.

Economic and Leadership Empowerment

2. *Capacity Building Programs:*

   - Women are trained in **income-generating activities** such as tailoring, appliqué work, and food processing.
   - Leadership and entrepreneurship workshops are conducted to encourage girls to take ownership of their futures.

Transforming Education Through Innovation

3. *Counseling and Guidance Services:*
   - A **dedicated counseling department** offers support to adolescent girls, addressing personal, academic, and societal challenges.
   - Special sessions focus on self-esteem, decision-making, and career planning.
4. *Representation in Classrooms and Beyond:*
   - Girls at KISS outshine in academics, sports, and cultural programs.
   - Their participation in **national and international platforms** like **UNICEF, UNESCO,** and **Women Empowerment Forums** highlights their transformation.

Example: Girls from KISS represented India at the **UN Permanent Forum on Indigenous Issues** in New York, showcasing their unique perspectives and achievements.

Action Research and Advocacy for Women's Empowerment

Prof. Samanta also emphasizes the role of teachers and researchers in driving change. Teachers at KISS are encouraged to:
- Conduct **action research** focusing on women's mobility, capacity building, and empowerment.
- Exchange experiences with national and international institutions to strengthen strategies for gender equity.

Cultural Empowerment Through Inclusion

KISS integrates girls into cultural preservation initiatives, recognizing the role of women as cultural custodians.
- Girls actively participate in **tribal dance, music, and storytelling** programs, ensuring the transmission of traditions to future generations.

Core Philosophy

Recognizing that women empowerment is the cornerstone of sustainable societal development, Prof. Achyuta Samanta has made it a mission to ensure that education reaches the most marginalized groups, particularly tribal girls. He firmly believes that **education transforms girls from 'liabilities' into 'assets'**, enabling them to become leaders and change agents within their communities.

Transforming Girls into Change Agents

Through its innovative teaching methods, holistic support systems, and dedicated efforts, KISS has succeeded in turning tribal girls into **confident, self-reliant, and capable individuals**. These young women return to their communities as **change agents**, breaking the cycle of poverty and discrimination.

Inspirational Tagline of him

"Educate a girl, empower a generation, and uplift a nation."

In His Words:

"Educate a girl, empower a generation, and uplift a nation. When a tribal girl finds her voice through education, an entire community finds its future. Empowerment begins with dignity, and dignity begins with opportunity."
— *Prof. Achyuta Samanta*

Conclusion

In the visionary outlook of Prof. Achyuta Samanta, education is far more than the transfer of knowledge—it is a transformative force that reshapes lives, uplifts communities, and drives societal progress. He believes that the aims of education should be dynamic, inclusive, and deeply rooted in the cultural, social, and economic realities of the people it serves. By addressing the holistic needs of students—intellectual, emotional, social, and spiritual—education can unlock their potential and enable them to become agents of change.

Prof. Samanta's educational philosophy stands as a beacon of hope and progress, particularly for marginalized and underprivileged communities. From fostering employability and life skills to preserving cultural heritage, empowering women, and nurturing creativity, his vision integrates traditional values with modern aspirations. It reflects his unwavering commitment to an equitable world where education becomes a tool for empowerment and a bridge to opportunity.

As he profoundly asserts, **"The aim of education is not just to meet the needs of today but to create the possibilities of tomorrow."** This transformative philosophy inspires KISS to redefine education as a holistic journey—one that shapes not only individuals but also the future of society as a whole. Through this progressive vision, Prof. Samanta proves that education is indeed the cornerstone of a just, inclusive, and sustainable world.

Curriculum

In Prof. Samanta's educational system at KISS, the curriculum stands as a cornerstone of the institution, designed not only to address the unique needs of tribal students but also to meet the broader societal demands. It reflects a progressive approach that aligns with the philosophy of holistic education, which integrates multiple aspects of human development—intellectual, emotional, social, and spiritual—into the learning process. Prof. Samanta views education as a means to nurture the whole child, fostering their natural development and potential.

At KISS, the curriculum is flexible and dynamic, not fixed, allowing for a personalized learning journey that takes into account each child's individual needs, interests, and aptitudes. The curriculum is child-centered, enabling students to engage in experiences that enhance their natural growth and development, creating a learning environment where they can thrive as individuals. Prof. Samanta believes that education should cater to all aspects of a child's being, empowering them not only with academic knowledge but also with life skills, values, and a sense of responsibility towards themselves, their community, and the world at large.

Thus, the curriculum at KISS is a fusion of academic rigor and practical skills, promoting an environment where students grow intellectually, emotionally, and socially, in alignment with the principles of holistic education. Through this approach, Prof. Samanta aims to equip tribal students with the tools necessary for navigating modern society while staying connected to their roots and cultural heritage. The following sections will delve deeper into the elements of the curriculum, which encapsulate the essence of holistic education in Prof. Samanta's vision.

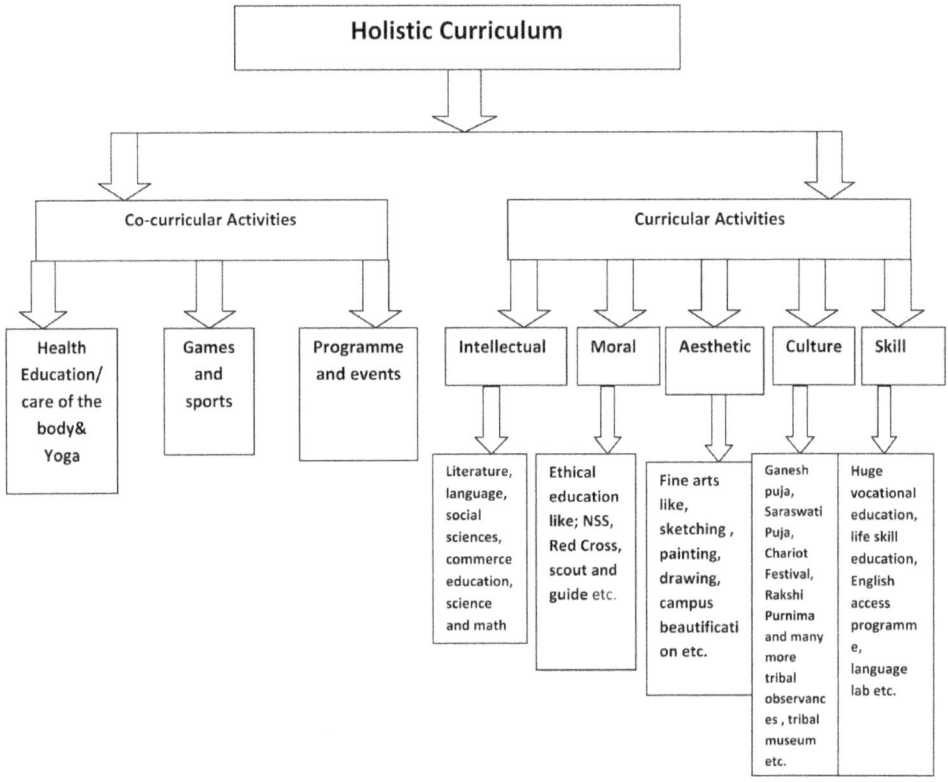

Common Syllabus for All-Round Development

One of the most important aspects of the curriculum at KISS is its comprehensive and inclusive approach to education, designed to ensure the all-round development of every student. Prof. A. Samanta, with a vision for a holistic educational system, introduced a common syllabus pattern that aligns with national education standards, while also considering the specific needs of the tribal students at KISS.

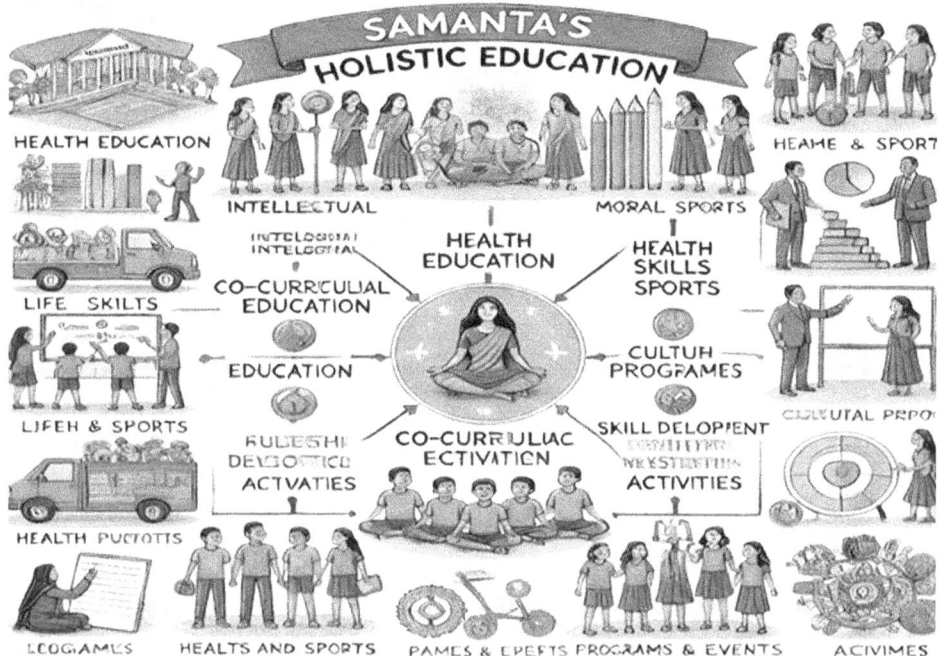

Understanding the diverse and vulnerable backgrounds of the 25,000 students at KISS, Prof. Samanta envisioned a curriculum that would provide them with equal opportunities to excel alongside students from other educational institutions. To achieve this, the institution offers a range of streams — Arts, Science, and Commerce — tailored to meet both the interests of students and the needs of the nation.

1. **Arts Stream:**

The Arts stream offers subjects such as Political Science, Economics, History, Sociology, Psychology, and Information Technology. These subjects empower students with a well-rounded understanding of the world, providing them with critical thinking and analytical skills.

2. **Science Stream:**

The Science stream includes subjects like Physics, Chemistry, Mathematics, Zoology, and Botany. This allows students to delve into the scientific realm, developing problem-solving skills and a solid foundation for future scientific research and careers.

3. **Commerce Stream:**

In the Commerce stream, students can study subjects like Accounting, Costing, Business Law, and Auditing. This equips them with the practical knowledge and skills needed for the business world, preparing them for various career paths in finance, management, and entrepreneurship.

Prof. Samanta's vision extends beyond undergraduate education. He has also introduced a wide array of **degree and post-graduate programs** that cater to the intellectual needs and ambitions of tribal students. The degree programs offered at KISS include subjects such as Psychology, Sociology, History, Education, Home Science, Business Administration, Social Science, Anthropology, and more. These programs provide students with the expertise and credentials to thrive in a competitive world.

In the post-graduate programs, students have the opportunity to specialize in subjects such as Physics, Chemistry, Mathematics, Zoology, Computer Science, Political Science, Economics, Philosophy, Sociology, and Odia. By offering such a diverse range of subjects, Prof. Samanta ensures that KISS students are well-equipped to compete with their peers not only in India but on a global scale.

Prof. Samanta's emphasis on a common syllabus reflects his unwavering belief that education must enable every child to thrive, regardless of their background. It is designed not just for academic achievement, but for the overall development of the students, preparing them to contribute meaningfully to society and the world. Through this holistic educational approach, KISS is bridging the gap between tribal students and mainstream society, empowering them to compete, innovate, and lead in the global arena.

The curriculum is not just a reflection of academic excellence but a testament to Prof. Samanta's enduring commitment to the empowerment of tribal children. It embodies his philosophy of education as a tool for transformation and a path to brighter futures for the underprivileged.

Vocational Education

Prof. Samanta has always emphasized the importance of vocational education as a vital component of the holistic development of students at KISS. Recognizing the rapidly changing demands of the modern world, he believes that education should not only focus on theoretical knowledge but also equip students with practical skills that will empower them to succeed in life and contribute meaningfully to society. With this vision, he has introduced a wide range of vocational courses, designed to cater to the diverse interests and abilities of the tribal students at KISS.

In line with the evolving educational landscape, Prof. Samanta emphasizes that vocational education is not just an alternative to traditional academic paths but an essential part of a balanced education. It provides students with the necessary skills and competencies to thrive in a rapidly developing job market, while also fostering entrepreneurship and self-reliance.

The vocational courses offered at KISS cover a variety of fields, ensuring that each student can find a trade that aligns with their personal interests and talents. These courses are tailored to meet both the needs of the students and the demands of the contemporary job market. The wide array of vocational training includes:

1. Computer Training
2. Composite Farming
3. Food Processing
4. Animal Husbandry
5. Art and Craft
6. Tailoring
7. Appliqué
8. Making Soft Toys
9. Chemical Works (e.g., phenyl, hand wash, dish wash)
10. Recycled Paper Production
11. Painting
12. Photo Framing
13. Incense Stick Making
14. Food Processing and Preservation
15. Medical Attendant Training
16. Security Guard Training
17. Bakery
18. Pisciculture (Fish Farming)
19. Driving
20. Mineral Water Processing

At KISS, the principle is simple: **"At least one vocational course is necessary for every student."** Prof. Samanta's commitment to vocational education is grounded in the belief that practical skills are crucial for economic empowerment. He understands that vocational education is directly linked to productivity, both on a personal and national level.

The goal of these vocational programs is to ensure that every student leaves KISS equipped with not just academic qualifications but also the practical expertise necessary to secure a job and support themselves and their families. Prof. Samanta's approach aims to bridge the gap between education and employment, helping tribal students transform into skilled professionals and entrepreneurs who can actively contribute to India's development.

Furthermore, vocational education at KISS is not merely about preparing students for immediate employment but also about fostering a sense of independence, confidence, and self-worth. By acquiring marketable skills, students are empowered to create their own opportunities, reducing dependence on external sources of income and enabling them to sustain a livelihood through their expertise.

Ultimately, Prof. Samanta envisions KISS as a place where vocational education plays a critical role in shaping the future of tribal students, turning them into not just employees, but leaders, innovators, and active participants in the socio-economic development of the nation. By equipping them with both academic knowledge and practical skills, KISS ensures that its students are ready to face the challenges of tomorrow and contribute to the greater good of society.

Training in Games and Sports

Sports and games play a crucial role in the holistic development of students, and at KISS, Prof. A. Samanta has emphasized their importance as part of a well-rounded educational experience. Recognizing the impact of physical development on the overall growth of individuals, he has ensured that sports are integrated into the curriculum as key co-curricular activities.

KISS offers a wide range of both indoor and outdoor sports, along with athletics, to cater to the diverse interests and talents of its students. The sports offered include Rugby football, football, cricket, volleyball, hockey, archery, chess, and many more. To ensure the highest level of training, professional coaches are appointed for each sport, providing expert guidance and coaching to help students develop their skills and excel in their chosen sports.

Prof. Samanta's vision for sports at KISS goes beyond just providing opportunities for physical fitness. He has created a robust infrastructure within the campus, offering world-class facilities for students to train and hone their abilities. Students are encouraged to participate in various competitions at the state, national, and international levels, with full support from the institution. This approach not only promotes the physical well-being of students but also nurtures their competitive spirit and self-confidence.

Sports at KISS are considered a major aspect of the co-curricular programme, and the impact is truly remarkable. Many students have gone on to achieve great success, both at the national and international levels. Notably, KISS students have qualified for the **Olympic Games**, and the institution's rugby team has earned the prestigious title of **World Champions**. These accomplishments are just a glimpse of the success stories emerging from KISS. The dedication to nurturing talent in the field of sports has also created multiple pathways for students to gain employment through the **sports quota** at national and state levels.

The training in sports at KISS goes far beyond winning medals or titles; it is about empowering students to realize their full potential, both physically and mentally. The lessons learned through sports — discipline, teamwork, leadership, resilience, and perseverance — are invaluable and serve students throughout their lives.

By offering top-tier sports training and guidance, Prof. Samanta has given students the tools to excel not only in academics but also in the arena of sports, creating opportunities for them to achieve success on the global stage. At KISS, sports are not just a means of recreation but a vital part of the institution's mission to cultivate well-rounded individuals who can contribute meaningfully to society.

The achievements of KISS students in the realm of sports stand as a testament to the vision and leadership of Prof. Samanta, whose unwavering commitment to the physical and mental development of his students has created champions both in the classroom and on the global sports stage. These accomplishments inspire the next generation of KISS students to dream big, work hard, and realize their potential as future leaders and athletes.

Games and Sports Trained at KISS:
1. **Football**
    - KISS provides football training with professional coaching, preparing students for state and national competitions.

2. **Rugby**
   - KISS is known for its exceptional rugby training program. The rugby team has achieved remarkable success, including winning international titles.
3. **Cricket**
   - Comprehensive cricket coaching is offered at KISS, with students participating in regional, national, and international cricket events.
4. **Volleyball**
   - KISS has a well-established volleyball program, with coaching support to help students excel at district and state levels.
5. **Hockey**
   - Hockey training is provided, and KISS students have represented at various levels, demonstrating their skills and sportsmanship.
6. **Archery**
   - KISS has produced accomplished archers who have competed in national and international competitions.
7. **Chess**
   - Chess is taught at KISS, with students frequently participating in and winning at national-level chess tournaments.
8. **Athletics**
   - KISS encourages participation in athletics, offering training in various track and field events such as sprints, long jump, high jump, and more.

9. **Badminton**
    - Students at KISS are trained in badminton, with opportunities to compete at state and national levels.
10. **Table Tennis**
    - Table tennis training is offered at KISS, producing skilled players who participate in state and national tournaments.
11. **Basketball**
    - KISS has a thriving basketball program, with students receiving rigorous training and participating in intercollegiate competitions.

Art and Craft Education

At KISS, education goes beyond theoretical learning, as it embraces the development of both physical and mental skills through Art and Craft education. Prof. Samanta Sir, a lover of beauty and nature, believes that fostering an aesthetic sense within students is essential for their overall development. To cultivate this appreciation for beauty, KISS offers a wide range of art and craft programs such as **painting, drawing, soft toys making, tailoring, weaving,** and more.

Prof. Samanta Sir understands that such creative pursuits not only engage the mind but also allow students to focus their attention and energy, thus enhancing their concentration and promoting mental well-being. Through art and craft education, students are able to nurture their creative thinking while simultaneously developing important moral and cultural values. By engaging in these hands-on activities, they gain a deeper connection to the world around them, fostering love and respect for nature and human expression.

One of Prof. Samanta's aims in offering such programs on a large scale is not only to provide a means of artistic and emotional expression but also to contribute to the institution's sustainability. The sale of art and craft materials helps meet some of the institution's expenses, with a portion of the proceeds being deposited into the artists' accounts. This initiative not only encourages self-reliance but also empowers students to see the value of their work.

Thus, through art and craft education, Prof. Samanta Sir has created an environment where students can flourish creatively, develop important life skills, and contribute to the institution while embracing the beauty and values of the world around them.

Multi-lingual Education

Multi-lingual education plays a crucial role in enhancing the educational experience for tribal children, helping them connect with their native languages while simultaneously gaining proficiency in multiple languages. This approach not only fosters a sense of identity and pride in their own language but also opens doors for better communication and broader opportunities.

At KISS, where over **30,000 students** from **62 tribal communities** and **13 primitive tribal groups** come together, language diversity is a unique challenge. These students, hailing from remote rural and tribal areas across India and beyond, speak a wide array of languages, including different

tribal dialects, **Hindi**, **Odia**, and **English**. Understanding the importance of language in the learning process, Prof. Samanta Sir recognized the need for a multi-lingual education system that would bridge these language gaps and create a more inclusive and harmonious learning environment.

To address these challenges, KISS has introduced multi-lingual education, providing a platform for students to learn and appreciate multiple languages. **Language teachers** specializing in **Santal, Munda, Soura,** and other tribal languages are appointed to teach and facilitate communication among students from different linguistic backgrounds. This approach helps students feel more at home, while also fostering a sense of belonging and community within the campus.

Prof. Samanta Sir's vision is to cultivate a **conducive atmosphere for learning**, where students can not only communicate but also engage meaningfully in their education. The multi-lingual approach ensures that students are not only equipped with the ability to communicate in their mother tongue but also gain proficiency in mainstream languages, enabling them to thrive in both their immediate communities and the broader world.

Recent examples of multi-lingual activities at KISS include **language exchange programs**, where students from different tribal backgrounds come together to share their languages and cultures. Additionally, **language proficiency workshops** are held regularly, where students learn **English, Hindi, and Odia**, and are encouraged to converse in multiple languages through group discussions, debates, and interactive exercises. This approach helps bridge cultural and linguistic divides while fostering mutual respect and understanding among the diverse student body.

Through this multi-lingual education system, Prof. Samanta Sir has created an inclusive and supportive environment where tribal children are not only able to preserve their cultural heritage but also acquire the language skills necessary to succeed in the modern world. It is a step toward breaking barriers, promoting inclusivity, and ensuring that these children are equipped to face global challenges while honoring their roots.

Language Education (with Language Lab) at KISS

Language is the cornerstone of communication, and for the diverse student body at KISS, language has played a pivotal role in bridging gaps and fostering learning. With over **30,000 students** from **62 tribal communities** and **13 primitive tribal groups**, the linguistic diversity at KISS presented a unique challenge. These students come from remote, rural, and tribal areas, each with its own distinct dialect, making it difficult to communicate and comprehend traditional languages of instruction such as **Odia, Hindi,** and **English.**

To address this challenge, **Prof. Samanta Sir** established a **Language Lab** at KISS, which serves as a powerful tool to overcome language barriers and facilitate effective communication and learning. Initially, the Language Lab focused on **four tribal languages**: **Santal**, **Soura**, **Munda**, and **Kandha**, which were taught to help students become familiar with these languages while also correlating them with **Odia**, **Hindi**, and **English**. This enabled tribal children to understand and relate to these mainstream languages by starting with their own mother tongue.

As new groups of tribal students joined the campus, **Desia** and **Juanga** languages were also introduced into the language lab, making the system even more inclusive. The primary goal of the language lab is to help students

who speak tribal dialects become comfortable with learning in **Odia, Hindi**, and **English**. The lab provides a seamless transition by enabling teachers to teach the students their subjects while converting their native dialects into these three languages during the **teaching-learning process**.

This innovative system ensures that the tribal children are not only able to **understand the subjects** they are being taught but also become proficient in **multiple languages**. With the **Language Lab**, students are able to grasp the core content of the lessons in a **language they are familiar with**, making it easier for them to transition to **Hindi, Odia, and English** over time.

The impact of the **Language Lab** is profound. It allows students to gain confidence in learning a new language while maintaining a strong connection to their cultural roots. This initiative has significantly contributed to **reducing dropout rates** at KISS, as students are motivated to continue their education in a setting where they feel comfortable and understood. The Language Lab not only helps them learn the subject matter but also aids them in adjusting to a new environment far from their homes, where they may face cultural and linguistic challenges.

Ultimately, the **Language Lab** at KISS is not just a tool for language learning, but also a bridge that connects **tribal children** to the wider world, empowering them to thrive academically and socially in an increasingly globalized society.

How the Language Lab Helps:
1. **Improved Communication Skills**: The Language Lab provides students with the opportunity to practice and improve their **speaking, listening, and writing skills** in a controlled and supportive environment. Students can engage with **audio-visual tools** and **interactive software** that help them refine their accent, vocabulary, and comprehension skills in a fun and engaging way.
2. **Overcoming Language Barriers**: For students who speak different tribal languages, the Language Lab helps them bridge the gap by offering **language tutorials** and **personalized coaching** in **Hindi, Odia**, and **English**. This ensures that students can engage with the curriculum and communicate confidently both within the school environment and in the outside world.
3. **Cultural Integration**: The Language Lab fosters cross-cultural communication by allowing students to explore and appreciate the linguistic diversity within their community. Through **peer interaction** and **language exchange sessions**, students learn not only to speak different languages but also to understand different cultural perspectives, thus fostering an inclusive atmosphere at KISS.
4. **Enhanced Academic Performance**: Mastery of languages like English and Hindi is essential for academic success, especially in fields such as **science**, **commerce**, and **arts**, where textbooks, resources, and exams are primarily conducted in these languages. The Language Lab empowers students by enhancing their **reading comprehension**, **writing ability**, and **spoken fluency**, contributing to better overall academic performance.
5. **Global Connectivity**: By developing proficiency in global languages like **English**, the Language Lab opens up opportunities for students to engage with the wider world. Students can access online learning platforms, participate in **international events**, and pursue further education or career opportunities beyond the local context.

Recent Activities in the Language Lab:
- **Language Workshops and Sessions**: The Language Lab organizes **regular workshops** where students engage in activities such as **debates, discussions**, and **role-plays** to practice communication in different languages. These interactive sessions not only improve fluency but also boost students' **confidence** in using the language in real-world scenarios.

- **Cultural and Linguistic Exchange Programs**: The Language Lab facilitates **language exchange** initiatives where students from different tribal backgrounds share their **native languages** with each other. This helps preserve tribal languages while simultaneously promoting **linguistic diversity** and **mutual respect**.
- **English Proficiency Classes**: Specialized **English language classes** are conducted in the Language Lab to enhance reading, writing, and speaking skills. These classes are tailored to the needs of tribal students, taking into consideration their language backgrounds and learning pace.
- **Multimedia Learning Tools**: The Language Lab utilizes a range of **audio-visual aids** such as **recorded lessons**, **language games**, and **interactive software** that help students develop a deeper understanding of language structures and usage.

Achievements:

- **Increased Language Proficiency**: Many students who initially faced challenges in speaking and understanding Hindi or English have shown remarkable progress. They are now able to **express themselves confidently** in these languages, contributing to classroom discussions and performing better academically.
- **Successful Participation in Competitions**: Students from KISS have excelled in various **language-based competitions**, such as **debates**, **elocution**, and **spelling bees**, at both state and national levels, demonstrating the effectiveness of the Language Lab.

In summary, the **Language Lab** at KISS is an invaluable resource that not only enhances **linguistic skills** but also promotes **cultural integration** and **academic excellence**. Through this initiative, Prof. Samanta Sir has ensured that the tribal students of KISS are well-equipped with the **language skills** necessary to succeed in the modern world, while also preserving their rich cultural heritage.

Life Skill Education

Life skill education has become a crucial aspect for the holistic development of adolescent boys and girls, helping them navigate the challenges of life effectively. Prof. Samanta Sir recognized the importance of shaping this critical stage of life, particularly in a large institution like KISS, where over **30,000 students** live and learn on a single campus. Adolescence, typically from ages **13 to 19**, is a transformative period that requires careful guidance and nurturing. At KISS, Prof. Samanta Sir has focused on equipping students with essential life skills that foster **self-discipline, positive thinking**, and a well-rounded approach to life.

In this regard, Prof. Samanta Sir introduced **Life Skill Education** as a key part of the curriculum. The core life skills training focuses on **ten essential skills** that are fundamental to personal and social development:

1. **Self Awareness**
2. **Empathy**
3. **Effective Communication**
4. **Interpersonal Relationships**
5. **Creative Thinking**
6. **Critical Thinking**
7. **Decision Making**
8. **Problem Solving**
9. **Dealing with Emotions**
10. **Coping with Stress**

The objective behind incorporating these skills into the curriculum is not only to help students lead better, more successful lives but also to equip them with the tools they need to handle the complexities of adolescence. The **goals** of the Life Skill Education initiative include:

- **Fostering creativity and positive thinking**
- **Promoting leadership qualities** and a sense of **social responsibility**
- Encouraging **healthy practices, personal hygiene**, and proper **nutrition**
- **Supporting reproductive health education** and fostering awareness of sexual health issues
- Teaching students how to **stay safe**, especially in situations of **harassment**, including **sexual harassment**
- **Managing peer pressure** and avoiding the dangers of **substance abuse**
- **Promoting social skills, gender sensitivity**, and respect for diversity
- Helping in **character building, social responsibility**, and **respect for justice**

As defined by the **World Health Organization (WHO)**, life skills are "abilities for adaptive and positive behavior that enable individuals to deal effectively with the demands and challenges of everyday life." In today's world, **psycho-social competencies**—skills that contribute to mental well-being—are vital for healthy development. Life skills foster **adaptive behavior** that helps individuals thrive in interactions with others and with their environment.

A key focus of life skill education at KISS is the **adolescent reproductive and sexual health education**, which is particularly relevant in the socio-cultural context. Prof. Samanta Sir has made it a priority to educate students on **personal hygiene**, **nutrition**, and how to address the challenges of **adolescent reproductive health**. This initiative not only provides students with valuable information on handling reproductive health issues but also creates a safe environment for them to discuss and understand the complexities of adolescence.

Life skill education at KISS goes beyond the theoretical; it includes real-world, hands-on activities that help students apply these skills in their daily lives. Recent activities have included **workshops** on **stress management**, **peer counseling**, and **leadership training**, along with campaigns focusing on **gender equality**, **mental health**, and **safe practices**. By incorporating these life skills into everyday learning, Prof. Samanta Sir ensures that the students are better prepared to face the challenges of life with confidence, resilience, and empathy.

Through the consistent and comprehensive approach to life skill education, Prof. Samanta Sir is nurturing a generation of students who are not only academically competent but also emotionally and socially adept, ready to contribute meaningfully to society and the world at large. This approach helps ensure that students at KISS grow into well-rounded individuals who can navigate life's challenges with strength, dignity, and a deep sense of responsibility.

Employment-Based Education

Prof. Samanta Sir envisions **self-reliance** as a fundamental aspect of modern life, especially for the tribal communities. He believes that for tribal children to successfully integrate into the mainstream society, it is essential to equip them with skills that foster independence and enable them to sustain themselves. At KISS, a strong emphasis is placed on **employment-based education**, providing students with a wide array of vocational training that ensures they are not only academically capable but also skilled in practical trades.

The **vocational education** offered at KISS includes a diverse range of skills such as **appliqué**, **candle making**, **sewing machine operation**, and more. These courses are designed to empower students to become self-reliant, enabling them to support their families and contribute to their communities once they complete their education. This approach not only imparts valuable skills but also helps meet the various operational needs of the institution itself.

In addition to vocational training, KISS also organizes **coaching classes** for students aiming to pursue higher achievements. These coaching sessions focus on preparing students for competitive exams such as **IAS, OAS, banking,** and **railway exams**. The coaching is provided by **experienced teachers** and **resource persons** from prestigious universities, as well as the **School of Leadership** at **KIIT University**. Prof. Samanta Sir initiated this valuable service because many tribal students come from economically disadvantaged backgrounds and cannot afford to seek external coaching. By offering these services within the campus, KISS ensures that students have the resources they need to compete at the state and national levels.

The primary aims behind these initiatives are twofold: firstly, to make education accessible and affordable for tribal students, allowing them to pursue their dreams without the financial burden of external coaching; and secondly, to help them **qualify for prestigious administrative services** at both the state and central levels. Prof. Samanta Sir's vision for **employment-based education** is to nurture students who are not only skilled workers but also capable individuals who can rise to leadership roles in various sectors, thereby contributing to the progress of their communities and the nation as a whole.

Through these efforts, Prof. Samanta Sir is building a bridge for tribal students to move from the margins to the mainstream, ensuring that they can become self-reliant, empowered, and influential citizens who will shape the future of India.

Micro-English Access Programme

The **Micro-English Access Programme** is an integral part of the expansive curriculum at the **Kalinga Institute of Social Sciences (KISS)**. Prof. Samanta Sir introduced this programme with a profound understanding of the importance of **English** in today's globalized world. English is not just an international language but also a vital tool for **trade and commerce, official communication**, and **higher education**. In India, it serves as the medium of instruction in many academic and professional fields. Therefore, proficiency in speaking, reading, and writing in English is crucial, particularly for tribal students, to bridge the gap between their traditional knowledge and the modern world.

One of the most significant challenges faced by tribal students is their initial fear and resistance to learning English. For many, English is seen as a foreign language, drastically different from their mother tongues, making it difficult to embrace. Prof. Samanta Sir, understanding this psychological barrier, designed the **Micro-English Access Programme** to gradually develop fluency in English. The aim is to build **speaking, reading, and writing skills** among the students, fostering their confidence and breaking the mental block that often surrounds the language.

The programme is structured to provide **intensive language training**, with a special focus on **communicative English**, which is crucial for real-world interactions. Prof. Samanta Sir recognized that in order to thrive in higher education and the professional world, tribal students must be equipped with the ability to communicate effectively in English. To achieve this, the programme ensures that **all students** attend the classes regularly, emphasizing the practical use of the language in daily life and academic contexts.

This initiative reflects Prof. Samanta Sir's deep commitment to the **holistic development** of tribal students, integrating language learning as a vital component of their overall education. The programme not only aims to enhance **linguistic skills** but also seeks to empower students to face the challenges of a rapidly changing world with **confidence** and **competence**.

By making **English language proficiency** a mandatory part of the curriculum, Prof. Samanta Sir is preparing tribal children not just to succeed academically but to **engage with the world** in meaningful ways. This initiative helps them **overcome linguistic barriers**, **enhance their cognitive abilities**, and ultimately **empower them** to participate fully in the global economy, thus ensuring a brighter future for them and their communities.

Cultural Education

Culture is the **way of life** and the **mirror of our society**. It represents the **identity** and values that shape a community. At **Kalinga Institute of Social Sciences (KISS)**, where over **30,000 tribal students** are receiving education, culture plays a central role in their lives. Each tribe has its own distinct cultural traditions, rituals, and practices, which are integral to their identity. Prof. Samanta Sir understood the significance of nurturing and preserving these rich cultural heritages while ensuring that the students are integrated into the broader national society.

One of the core principles of **Prof. Samanta Sir's educational philosophy** is the belief that cultural observances are not just personal or communal, but

essential to the **psychological well-being** and **sense of belonging** of the students. He realized that disconnecting tribal students from their cultural roots would hinder their ability to thrive in a diverse society, making them feel alienated. Therefore, Prof. Samanta Sir ensured that the students at KISS were encouraged to **celebrate and uphold their cultural traditions** within the institution.

In KISS, students are given the freedom and opportunity to participate in various cultural activities and observances that reflect their tribal traditions. These activities include traditional dances, music, arts, and festivals that are significant to their communities. Along with the cultural observances specific to each tribe, Prof. Samanta Sir also introduced the celebration of national festivals such as **Independence Day**, **Republic Day**, **Ganesh Puja**, **Saraswati Puja**, and the **Chariot Festival**. The goal was not only to celebrate the cultural diversity of India but also to **mainstream tribal students**, fostering a sense of unity and national pride while respecting their individual cultural identities.

Prof. Samanta Sir's objective was never simply to observe cultural practices but to **preserve them** for future generations. By integrating **tribal culture** with broader societal observances, he ensured that KISS remained a place where students could celebrate their heritage while embracing the values of a democratic and inclusive society. His vision was to create an environment where students felt free to express their cultural identity without fear of discrimination or loss of connection with their roots.

In this way, **Cultural Education** at KISS serves as a bridge—linking the students' **ancestral wisdom** with modern educational practices, ensuring that they are not only educated but also empowered to preserve and celebrate their cultural heritage for generations to come. This approach nurtures the **holistic development** of the students, reinforcing the importance of both **individuality** and **unity**, and ultimately contributing to a more inclusive and diverse society.

Health Education & Care of the Body: A Foundation for Lifelong Well-being

Growing up in extreme poverty, Prof. Samanta understood that lack of health awareness and medical care often became barriers to education. He realized that to uplift marginalized communities, it was essential to:

- Provide proper nutrition to ensure students' physical and cognitive growth.
- Create awareness about hygiene and preventive healthcare to reduce disease and absenteeism.
- Ensure access to quality medical care to safeguard students' well-being.

How KISS Implements His Vision:
- **Free Medical Check-ups & Healthcare Facilities** – Every student receives routine health check-ups and free treatment, ensuring a healthy learning environment.
- **Balanced Nutrition for All** – KISS provides three nutritious meals a day, designed to combat malnutrition and enhance physical and mental development.
- **Hygiene & Sanitation Awareness** – From childhood, students are taught the importance of personal hygiene, clean drinking water, and sanitation as a daily practice.
- **Mental Health & Counseling Support** – Recognizing the emotional struggles that many children face, KISS has dedicated counselors who provide psychological guidance and mental well-being programs.

"A healthy student is a better learner. Without a strong foundation in health, education remains incomplete." – Prof. Achyuta Samanta

Yoga & Meditation: Strengthening the Mind & Soul
- Prof. Samanta has always emphasized the importance of mental well-being in education. He firmly believes that:
- Yoga enhances focus and memory, improving academic performance.
- Meditation promotes emotional balance, helping students overcome stress.
- Self-discipline through yoga builds a strong foundation for life.

How KISS Implements His Vision:
- **Daily Yoga Practice** – Every morning, students participate in guided yoga sessions, improving concentration, flexibility, and energy levels.
- **Meditation for Emotional Well-being** – Special mindfulness programs are integrated to help students manage stress, anxiety, and emotional challenges.
- **Participation in National & International Yoga Events** – KISS students have represented India in global yoga events, promoting its benefits worldwide.

- **Yoga as a Life Skill** – Beyond physical benefits, yoga at KISS instills patience, self-discipline, and inner strength, preparing students for life beyond academics.

"A peaceful mind is a powerful mind. Yoga is not just an exercise; it is a way to live life with balance and purpose." – Prof. Achyuta Samanta

Methods of Teaching

Prof. Samanta Sir firmly believes that traditional methods of teaching, which focus on rote memorization and passive learning, are neither democratic nor engaging for students. These outdated methods do not stimulate the intellectual curiosity or creativity needed to prepare students for the challenges of the modern world. Education, according to Prof. Samanta Sir, should not be confined to mere cramming of facts. It should be a **dynamic and interactive process**, designed to cultivate a deeper understanding, foster critical thinking, and promote **active participation**.

Many prominent educationists and philosophers have advocated for various teaching methods, each shaped by the context of their time and the needs of society. From the **lecture method** to the **heuristic method**, the evolution of teaching methods has been influenced by a desire to make learning more meaningful and engaging. In this global context, Prof. Samanta Sir recognized the limitations of autocratic teaching methods and instead adopted a range of **modern, democratic, and learner-centered approaches**.

He embraced teaching strategies that encourage students to actively participate in their learning process, focusing on methods that align with the **interests**, **inclinations**, and **capacities** of the child. These methods foster a **student-centered environment**, where children are not passive recipients of knowledge but active participants in their educational journey. Prof. Samanta Sir integrated the following modern teaching methods in his educational philosophy:

1. **Play-way Method**: Learning through play is a natural and engaging way for young children to grasp complex concepts. This method allows students to learn in a relaxed, joyful environment, stimulating their creativity, and cognitive development.
2. **Heuristic Method**: This method encourages students to discover knowledge through their own experience and problem-solving. It promotes **inquiry-based learning**, where students explore, hypothesize, and test ideas, developing critical thinking skills in the process.
3. Experiential and Active Learning: Hands-on learning enables students to understand concepts by actively engaging in practical tasks. This

method aligns with the belief that **learning is most effective when it is directly connected to real-life experiences**.
4. **Problem-Solving Method**: Prof. Samanta Sir believes that education should prepare students to face the challenges of life. The problem-solving method helps students develop analytical and logical thinking by tackling real-world problems and coming up with creative solutions.
5. **Project Method**: Learning through projects helps students delve deep into a particular subject, allowing them to research, collaborate, and apply their knowledge in practical contexts. This method encourages **critical thinking, creativity**, and **teamwork**.
6. **Maxims of Teaching**: Prof. Samanta Sir also emphasized the application of time-tested **principles of teaching**, such as starting from the known to the unknown, making the subject matter relevant to students, and ensuring active participation in the learning process.

Prof. Samanta Sir's approach to teaching reflects his **vision of holistic education**, where the focus is not just on academic achievement but also on the **overall development** of the child—emotionally, socially, and intellectually. He understood that when students are motivated, when their interests and natural inclinations are honored, they engage more deeply with the material and develop a lifelong love for learning. In this way, the teaching methods adopted by Prof. Samanta Sir stimulate curiosity, promote **cooperation** between students and teachers, and foster **empathy** and **fellow-feeling** among peers.

By rejecting the outdated, autocratic methods of the past, Prof. Samanta Sir created an educational environment where students are **empowered** to take charge of their learning, explore new ideas, and develop the critical thinking and problem-solving skills they need to thrive in the world. His **innovative methods** reflect his belief in the **democratic nature** of education—one where each child's voice, potential, and individuality are respected and nurtured.

This philosophy is not just about imparting knowledge; it's about cultivating an environment where students are encouraged to **grow as holistic individuals**, equipped to face the challenges of the future with confidence, creativity, and a sense of social responsibility.

Play-Way Method: A Path to Holistic Education

The term *"play-way"* was first introduced by Coldwell Cook to describe his innovative approach to teaching English. Inspired by the same philosophy, **Prof. Achyuta Samanta**, the visionary behind Kalinga Institute of Social

Sciences (KISS), has embraced the play-way method to nurture a joyful and engaging learning environment. Recognizing that the spirit of childhood is rooted in play, this method emphasizes child-centered education, advocating for learning through activities that allow children to immerse themselves wholeheartedly in an atmosphere of freedom, creativity, and spontaneity.

Prof. Samanta often says, *"Education should be fun, not forced."* He believes that any activity undertaken in the spirit of joy transcends the concept of work. Conversely, activities devoid of this spirit become burdensome and uninspiring. Guided by this belief, KISS has woven the play-way approach into its educational fabric, aligning it with the broader goals of holistic education.

Play-Way at KISS: Transforming Learning into Joyful Exploration

At KISS, the play-way method is not limited to a teaching strategy; it is a way of fostering intellectual curiosity, emotional well-being, and cultural pride. This approach is rooted in holistic education, which seeks to develop every aspect of a child's personality—physical, mental, emotional, social, and moral.

Prof. Samanta's vision emphasizes activities such as hobbies, dramatization, scouting, excursions, and self-governance, which serve as dynamic tools to make education lively and impactful. These activities underscore a critical lesson: education reaches its highest potential when it inspires enthusiasm and joy.

Integrating Play into the Curriculum

Throughout the academic year, teachers at KISS use playful methods to create meaningful learning experiences. For instance:
- **Stage Plays**: Used to teach history and mother tongue, helping students understand concepts through dramatized storytelling.

- **Mathematical Games**: Designed to teach and practice mathematical facts in an interactive manner.
- **Competitions**: Group activities, such as vocabulary-building contests or quizzes, stimulate students' interest in subjects ranging from language to general knowledge.

These strategies ensure that students actively participate in their learning, fostering intrinsic motivation and sustained interest.

Examples of Playful Activities at KISS
For Primary Students:
1. **Picture Recognition:** Enhances observation and memory.
2. **Matching Boards:** Builds logical reasoning and association skills.
3. **Flashcards:** Introduces foundational concepts in an engaging manner.
4. **Word Building and Spelling Games:** Develops language skills in a collaborative setting.
5. **Finding the Odd One Out:** Encourages critical thinking.
6. **Sentence Construction:** Enhances grammar and creativity.

Games for Middle Classes: Engaging Minds Through Play

Holistic education emphasizes the all-round development of a child — intellectual, emotional, social, and moral. At KISS, various games are tailored to middle school students, not just to impart knowledge but also to nurture creativity, teamwork, and problem-solving skills. These games create an engaging learning environment where students actively participate and connect lessons with real-life experiences.

1. **The Story Game**

Storytelling is a powerful tool in holistic education, as it combines imagination, empathy, and critical thinking. In this game, the teacher introduces a topic through a story that contains key facts or concepts. After listening, students are encouraged to relate the story to similar events in their own lives.

- **Holistic Impact:** Enhances listening skills, encourages personal reflection, and fosters emotional intelligence by connecting academic concepts with personal experiences.

2. **The Description Game**

This game emphasizes teamwork and communication. The class is divided into two groups. Each group selects a specific topic or object but keeps it a secret from one member, who is designated as the "stranger." Group members then provide clues, one by one, to help the stranger deduce the topic. If the stranger fails to guess, another student provides a new clue.

- **Holistic Impact:** Builds deductive reasoning, strengthens verbal communication, and encourages collaboration while promoting an atmosphere of fun and mutual respect.

3. **The Question Game**

In this game, the class is split into teams that take turns answering questions posed by the teacher or peers. Points are awarded for correct answers, and the group with the highest score wins. The questions can cover a wide range of topics, from academics to general knowledge.

- **Holistic Impact:** Encourages healthy competition, sharpens cognitive abilities, and develops a love for inquiry and critical thinking, all while fostering social skills and teamwork.

4. **The Missing Term Game**

This game challenges students to think logically and connect ideas. The teacher provides a pair of related terms (e.g., "sun: day") and then offers a partial pair (e.g., "moon: ___"). Students must fill in the blank with the correct term ("night"). The game can be adapted to subjects like mathematics, science, or language.

- **Holistic Impact:** Improves logical reasoning, enhances vocabulary, and strengthens pattern recognition while promoting mental agility and confidence.

Examples of Playful Activities at KISS for Higher Classes

1. **Debate Competitions and Group Discussions**

   Students engage in debates and group discussions on current affairs, social issues, and academic topics, enhancing their critical thinking, communication skills, and confidence.

2. **Subject-Specific Quizzes**

Interactive quizzes in subjects like science, mathematics, and history challenge students' knowledge and foster a spirit of healthy competition while reinforcing classroom learning.

3. **Science Experiments and Project-Based Learning**

Students conduct experiments and work on projects that connect theory with practical applications, nurturing problem-solving skills and creativity.

4. **Role-Playing and Creative Writing**

Role-playing activities and creative writing exercises allow students to explore diverse perspectives and improve their analytical and imaginative abilities.

5. **Workshops in Technology and Robotics**

Technology and robotics workshops equip students with modern technical skills, making them future-ready and fostering an innovative mindset.

6. **Field Trips and Exploration Tasks**

Visits to museums, industries, and ecological sites encourage experiential learning, boosting awareness and interest in real-world applications of academic concepts.

7. **Dramatization and Skits**

Performing skits and role-plays on historical and literary themes helps students internalize lessons, improve public speaking, and develop teamwork.

8. **Cultural Activities**

Music, dance, and painting competitions celebrate tribal heritage and creative expression while promoting cultural appreciation and self-confidence.

9. **Entrepreneurship and Life Skills Training**

Workshops on entrepreneurship and vocational skills help students learn practical knowledge for self-reliance and career readiness.

10. **Leadership and Social Responsibility Tasks**

Students take on leadership roles in organizing school events and participating in community service, fostering responsibility and organizational skills.

11. **Outdoor Games and Sports**

Sports and games are integral, teaching students discipline, teamwork, and resilience while promoting physical well-being.

12. **Environmental Conservation Activities**

Tree planting, waste management, and nature walks instill environmental consciousness and encourage sustainable practices among students.

These playful activities, woven into the academic curriculum, make learning dynamic and enjoyable, preparing KISS students for holistic growth and success.

Fostering Holistic Development Through Play

These games are more than just classroom activities—they are essential tools for holistic learning. By combining knowledge acquisition with skills like empathy, teamwork, and creative thinking, these activities prepare students for the challenges of real life. They also align with the KISS philosophy of making education engaging and meaningful, ensuring that learning becomes a joyful journey rather than a monotonous task.

Not only does the play-way method pave the way for effective and enduring education, but it also fulfills the broader aims of holistic education. By addressing the physical, mental, emotional, social, and moral dimensions of development, it nurtures the harmonious growth of children's personalities. Through playful and meaningful activities, it provides opportunities for behavioral refinement, helping students adapt to their environment and navigate life with confidence and resilience.

At KISS, this approach has transformed the learning experience. The campus fosters an engaging and joyful atmosphere where education is not a burden but a natural and enjoyable part of life. The absence of punitive control and the integration of innovative, student-centered pedagogy have resulted in exceptional retention rates. Moreover, KISS's educational model strengthens the indigenous knowledge of tribal children, preserving their rich cultural values while equipping them with modern technological skills.

Thus, the play-way method, as practiced at KISS, transcends conventional teaching. It becomes a bridge between tradition and modernity, fostering an education that is joyful, inclusive, and holistic. It exemplifies the profound truth that when education is rooted in play and purpose, it not only informs but transforms lives.

Inspirational tagline of him
"Learning with Joy, Growing with Play."

Heuristic Method: A Path to Discovery at KISS

In the words of Professor Armstrong, "The heuristic method of teaching involves placing students, as far as possible, in the attitude of a discoverer—encouraging them to find out things instead of merely being told." Originally introduced for teaching science, this method emphasizes discovery, experimentation, and independent research, making it an invaluable tool in fostering lifelong learners.

Prof. Achyuta Samanta, with his visionary approach to education, has seamlessly integrated the heuristic method at Kalinga Institute of Social Sciences (KISS). His aim is not just to teach students facts but to mold them into inquisitive thinkers and problem solvers, much like research scholars.

Implementation of the Heuristic Method at KISS

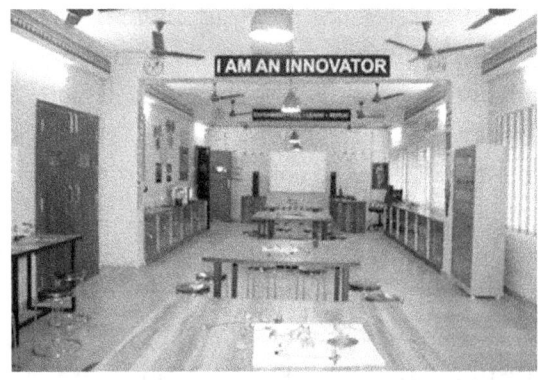

At KISS, a variety of activities and techniques reflect the principles of heuristic learning. For instance, students are provided with problem sheets containing minimal instructions and are guided to perform experiments or investigations related to the given problem. They document their observations, analyze their results, and draw conclusions, developing critical thinking and analytical skills in the process.

To ensure the success of this method, Prof. Samanta has introduced guiding principles for educators at KISS:

1. **Openness to Suggestions:** Teachers must be receptive to students' ideas and potential solutions, fostering an environment where creativity thrives.
2. **Patience over Quick Answers:** Teachers avoid providing immediate solutions, allowing students to explore and discover through persistence.
3. **Encouragement of Perseverance:** Students are reminded that the path to discovery and scientific thinking takes time, patience, and effort.
4. **Safe Space for Creativity:** Students are never ridiculed for unconventional or "silly" suggestions, ensuring their confidence remains intact.
5. **Guidance, Not Instruction:** Teachers act as facilitators, offering guidance only when absolutely necessary, empowering students to learn independently.
6. **Empathy and Preparation:** Teachers must be empathetic, courteous, and well-prepared to devise meaningful problems for students to investigate.

Infrastructure Supporting Heuristic Learning

To complement this method, KISS has developed extensive infrastructure that aligns with the principles of heuristic education. Some examples include:

- **Botanical Gardens:** Students conduct research and experiments related to plant biology and environmental conservation.

- **Mechanized Kitchens:** Students learn about efficient systems and the application of technology in daily life.
- **Bio-Gas Systems:** These provide hands-on experience in sustainable energy and environmental science.

- **Libraries and Laboratories:** A rich collection of resources enables in-depth exploration of various subjects.
- **Workshops:** Hands-on training in technical skills fosters creativity and innovation.

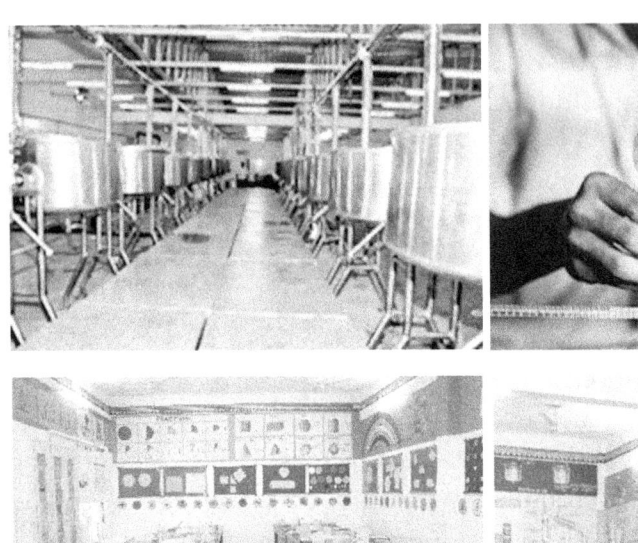
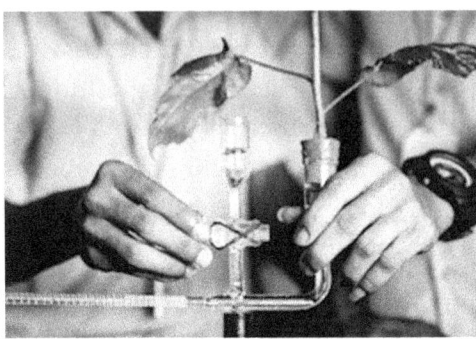

Benefits of the Heuristic Method

Through heuristic learning, students at KISS are not only gaining knowledge but are also developing essential life skills. Prof. Samanta's vision extends beyond academic learning, aiming to foster holistic growth in every student. The method achieves multiple objectives simultaneously:

1. **Psychological Development:** Students learn by self-practice, leading to deeper understanding and retention.

2. **Meaningful Learning:** Concepts are learned through personal experiences, leaving little room for forgetting.
3. **Self-Confidence and Discipline:** Students build confidence and discipline by taking ownership of their learning journey.
4. **Command over Subjects:** By actively engaging with the material, students develop a strong grasp of the subject matter.
5. **Interest and Willingness to Learn:** The method sparks curiosity and instills a love for learning.

The Vision of Prof. Samanta

By introducing the heuristic method, Prof. Samanta is not only providing scientific knowledge but also shaping well-rounded individuals. This approach aligns perfectly with the broader objectives of education at KISS, which include fostering self-reliance, critical thinking, and problem-solving skills among tribal children.

This method, infused with Prof. Samanta's dedication to blending traditional knowledge with modern pedagogy, makes learning at KISS both meaningful and transformative. Students leave with more than just academic success—they acquire the tools to navigate life's challenges with confidence and clarity.

Thus, the heuristic method stands as a testament to the educational philosophy of Prof. Achyuta Samanta, ensuring that education at KISS remains a beacon of hope, empowerment, and innovation for generations to come.

Inspirational tagline of him
"Empowering Minds to Explore, Experiment, and Excel."

Experiential and Active Learning: Experiencing Education Through Action at KISS

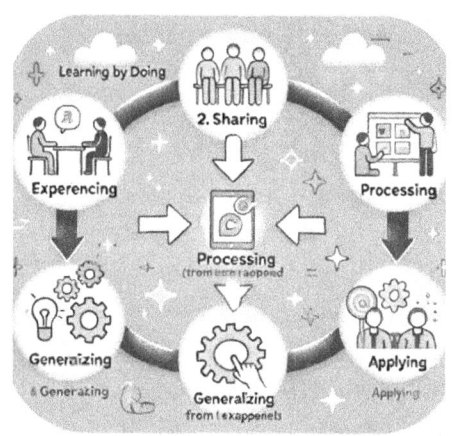

The essence of Experiential and Active Learning lies in enabling students to construct their own understanding of the world through active engagement and problem-solving. At Kalinga Institute of Social Sciences (KISS), the philosophy of experiential learning is brought to life through diverse opportunities ranging from technological to vocational education. Guided by the visionary leadership of Prof. Achyuta Samanta, KISS integrates this method across its pedagogy to ensure holistic development and life readiness for its students.

The benefits of Experiential and Active Learning

Prof. Samanta believes that education should not merely be theoretical but also practical and purposeful. Through this approach, students are empowered to:

1. Gain first-hand experience and practical knowledge.
2. Understand the value of hands-on activity.
3. Acquire skills for teamwork and group dynamics.
4. Develop critical thinking and problem-solving abilities.
5. Master the use of various tools and equipment.
6. Identify and address problems effectively.
7. Cultivate self-confidence, independence, and reliability.
8. Embrace values like honesty and responsibility, enriching their contributions to society.

Examples of Experiential Learning at KISS

1. **Student-Friendly Chemical Activities**

Students at KISS engage in creating everyday products such as soaps, candles, and bio-cleaners, which are used within the campus. This not only enhances their understanding of chemical processes but also instills entrepreneurial skills, aligning with Prof. Samanta's vision of self-reliance and sustainable livelihoods.

2. **Laboratories for Scientific Exploration**

Well-equipped laboratories cater to the vast number of students, encouraging them to experiment, research, and learn by doing. Students gain practical knowledge in science, acquiring skills that are integral to scientific discovery and application.

3. **Science Park for Environmental Learning**

KISS boasts a dedicated Science Park, where students explore medicinal plants, botanical gardens, and ecological systems. This hands-on engagement promotes environmental awareness alongside scientific learning, nurturing a sense of responsibility toward nature.

4. **Basic Life-Oriented Training**

Every student at KISS receives training in at least one livelihood skill, such as operating sewing machines, making appliqué crafts, agricultural techniques, or designing toys like teddy bears. These programs inspire creativity and prepare students for self-sustained lives after their education.

Experiential and Active Learning in Practice @ KISS

Primary Level

Teachers ensure activities are tailored to the age and understanding of young learners. For instance, a lesson on solubility might involve students dissolving sugar or salt in water, observing, and recording results, thus engaging them fully in the learning process.

Middle School Level

Students are encouraged to undertake independent projects such as collecting metal and non-metal objects or curating historically significant items like stamps. This promotes research skills and reinforces concepts through personal exploration.

Examples of Experiential and Active Learning **Activities at KISS for Higher Classes**

1. **Hands-On Science Projects**

   Students perform experiments in well-equipped laboratories, such as studying chemical reactions, physics demonstrations, or biology dissections, to better understand theoretical concepts through direct application.

2. **Technology Integration Tasks**

   Students engage in creating digital presentations, editing videos, and programming in computer labs, integrating their learning with practical technological tools essential for the modern world.

3. **Community-Based Activities**

   Students participate in activities like conducting surveys in local communities, organizing health camps, or environmental clean-ups, fostering social responsibility and practical knowledge.

4. **Agricultural Training**

   Practical sessions in agriculture, including soil testing, organic farming techniques, and irrigation methods, connect students with sustainable practices and self-reliance.

5. **Engineering and Craft Projects**

    Students design and build small-scale models such as bridges, machines, or architectural layouts, developing problem-solving and creative skills.

6. **Cultural Preservation Efforts**

    Hands-on training in tribal arts, crafts, and dances allows students to preserve their heritage while learning the importance of cultural identity and artistry.

7. **Eco-Friendly Practices**

    Practical involvement in bio-gas systems, waste management, and gardening activities teaches sustainable living practices and environmental conservation.

8. **Vocational Training**

Students receive hands-on training in skills such as tailoring, carpentry, or food processing, providing them with valuable entrepreneurial opportunities post-education.

9. **Mathematical Applications in Real Life**

Activities such as constructing geometric models or calculating real-life statistics instill a deeper understanding of mathematical concepts.

10. **Entrepreneurial Exercises**

Simulations such as setting up a mock business or creating marketing plans encourage innovative thinking and understanding of economic systems.

These activities ensure that KISS students not only gain academic knowledge but also practical skills, fostering a sense of confidence and preparing them for real-life challenges.

Holistic Impact of Experiential and Active Learning

The Experiential and Active Learning approach at KISS goes beyond academics. It addresses multiple dimensions of education, fostering creativity, environmental consciousness, teamwork, and practical knowledge. It equips students with life skills and nurtures a generation of confident, competent, and compassionate individuals who are ready to face the challenges of the modern world.

Inspirational tagline of him
"Transforming Lives Through Action and Experience."

Problem Solving: Nurturing Critical Thinkers at KISS

In everyday life, a problem is often seen as an obstacle or difficulty, but in education, it is an opportunity to question, explore, and innovate. Webster's Dictionary defines a problem as "a question raised for inquiry, consideration, or solution." True problem solving involves applying an unknown method to a novel situation under specific conditions, aiming for a meaningful and satisfactory solution.

At its core, problem-solving is about transforming the current state (the *now-state*) into a desired future state (the *goal-state*). It is a process where creativity and critical thinking combine to improve the quality of life. In education, problem-solving helps students actively engage with real-life challenges, equipping them with skills for a lifetime of learning.

Inspired by this vision, **Prof. Samanta Sir** has championed the problem-solving approach at KISS, recognizing its profound impact on students' lives. He continuously guides teachers in implementing this method effectively. His philosophy includes the following principles:

1. **Modeling a Problem-Solving Method**

Teachers articulate their methods while solving problems, enabling students to observe, compare, and connect strategies. This inspires students to adopt a structured approach.

2. **Teaching Within Specific Contexts**

Real-life problems are incorporated into lessons, examples, and assignments. Prof. Samanta emphasizes avoiding abstract problem-solving lessons, instead grounding them in meaningful, relatable scenarios.

3. **Helping Students Understand the Problem**

He advises teachers to focus on the *what* and *why* of a problem, as clarity in these areas makes the *how* of problem-solving significantly easier for students to grasp.

4. **Providing Adequate Time**

Teachers are encouraged to allocate ample time for students to understand problems, define goals, collaborate, make and correct mistakes, and fully solve problems within a single session whenever possible.

5. **Asking Questions and Offering Suggestions**

Teachers engage students with probing questions and strategic suggestions, fostering reflection on the approaches used in problem-solving and

encouraging independent thinking.
  6. **Linking Errors to Misconceptions**
Prof. Samanta stresses the importance of isolating and correcting misconceptions. Teachers guide students to learn from their mistakes, turning errors into valuable lessons that strengthen their understanding.

Problem-Solving in Action at KISS

At KISS, problem-solving is embedded in various activities across disciplines:

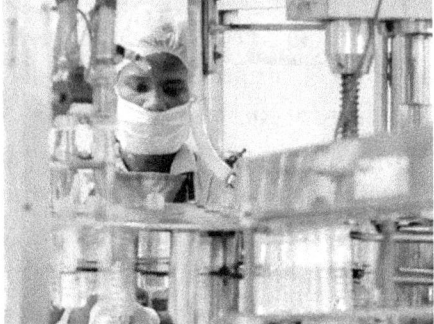

- In **science labs**, students conduct experiments to resolve real-world challenges, such as water purification or renewable energy models.
- Through **community service initiatives**, students identify and address societal issues, developing empathy and practical skills.

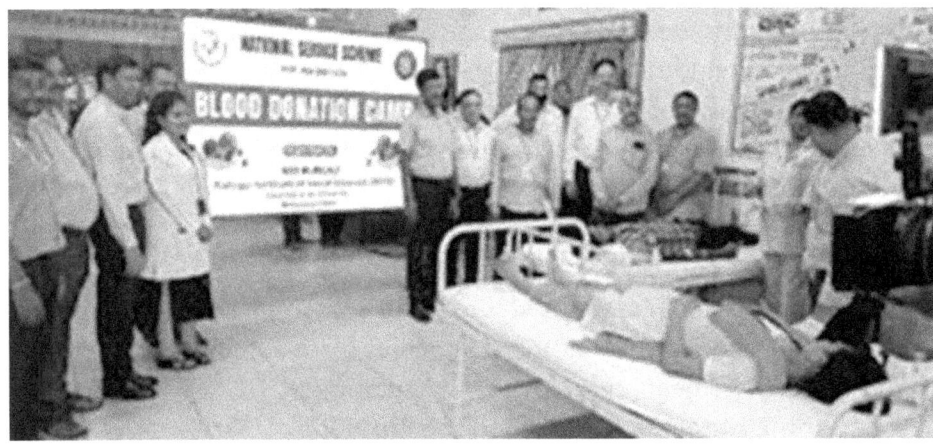

- In **entrepreneurial workshops**, students brainstorm solutions for creating sustainable livelihoods, integrating creativity with economic awareness.

This approach not only equips students with critical thinking skills but also fosters self-confidence, resilience, and a problem-solving mindset essential for thriving in any field.

Inspirational tagline of him
"Empowering Minds to Transform Challenges into Opportunities."

Project Method: Cultivating Innovation and Collaboration at KISS

William H. Kilpatrick, known as "Mr. Project Method," described a project as "a wholehearted, purposeful activity proceeding in a social environment." A project is not just a task; it is a planned and meaningful experience designed to unfold in a collaborative and dynamic setting, helping students connect learning with life.

At KISS, **Prof. Samanta Sir** has embraced this method as a cornerstone of education, emphasizing its ability to prepare students for life—not in some distant future, but here and now. He inspires educators to incorporate projects that are purposeful, creative, and socially relevant, fostering a holistic and experiential learning process.

Implementation of the Project Method at KISS

1. **Science Fairs and Exhibitions**

Students are encouraged to design and develop innovative projects for science fairs held within the campus and beyond. These projects often explore real-world applications, ranging from renewable energy solutions to models addressing local environmental challenges. KISS students also participate in state, national, and international science exhibitions, showcasing their ideas and learning from peers across the globe.

2. **Campus Beautification Projects**

To instill a sense of ownership and creativity, students are grouped to work on beautifying the vast KISS campus. Projects include planting medicinal trees, initiating horticultural practices, creating artistic installations, and painting murals. Each student contributes their unique ideas, transforming the campus into an inspiring and sustainable environment.

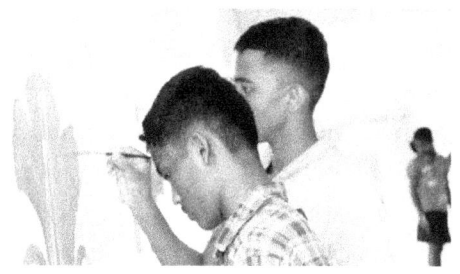

3. **Socially Relevant Projects**

Projects like developing community models for clean water, renewable energy, and waste management are undertaken, aligning education with social responsibility. This enables students to understand and contribute to the needs of their communities while learning practical skills.

4. **Collaborative Learning Culture**

Prof. Samanta emphasizes that teachers act as facilitators and mentors, creating a democratic and inclusive atmosphere. Teachers guide students while empowering them to take initiative, fostering teamwork and mutual respect. They understand each student's abilities and interests, assigning tasks accordingly to ensure active participation and meaningful learning.

By engaging in project-based learning, students at KISS cultivate creativity, problem-solving skills, leadership, and a sense of responsibility. This approach transforms classrooms into innovation hubs and prepares students for real-world challenges.

Inspirational tagline of him

"Building Innovators, One Project at a Time."

Maxims of Teaching: Activity-Based Learning for Meaningful Education

The Maxims of Teaching provide a structured approach for effective learning, emphasizing a progression from simple to complex, known to unknown, and concrete to abstract. Prof. Achyuta Samanta has adapted these maxims to the tribal context of KISS by embedding them into activity-based learning methods, ensuring education is practical, engaging, and impactful.

1. **Language Learning Through Familiar Contexts**

To bridge the language gap, teachers use activity-based methods like **vocabulary games** and **storytelling sessions** in native languages. For instance, students learn the English word "water" by relating it to terms like 'Pain' in Sambalpuri, 'Hani' in

Paraja, or 'Daa' in Ho. Activities like **role-playing in conversations** help them practice new words, making language learning both enjoyable and effective.

2. **Progressive Mathematics Skills Development**

Mathematics classes integrate activities such as **problem-solving worksheets** and **interactive quizzes**, starting with basic algebra and geometry. As students gain confidence, they tackle more complex concepts like integration and matrices. These activities build their skills step-by-step, turning abstract problems into engaging challenges.

3. **Hands-On Science Learning**

In science, teachers use **experiments and demonstrations** to move from concrete to abstract. For example, while teaching the digestive system, students work on **building models of the digestive tract** or observing the process through animations and experiments. These hands-on activities ensure students understand each component before synthesizing the overall system.

4. **Social Sciences Through Real-Life Exploration**

Social science classes incorporate **field visits** and **experiential activities**. When learning about the Jagannath Temple or campus medical facilities, students take guided tours to these places. They participate in activities like **documenting observations** or creating **visual presentations**, making their learning vivid and long-lasting.

5. **Testing and Tailored Learning Plans**

Teachers begin higher-level classes by conducting **diagnostic tests** to gauge students' prior knowledge. Based on results, personalized learning activities like **peer tutoring, group projects**, or **skill-building tasks** are designed to meet individual needs, ensuring no student is left behind.

6. **Environmental Learning Through Activities**

KISS integrates environmental education into daily learning. Activities such as **campus gardening, tree planting drives**, or **waste segregation programs** teach students about sustainability while giving them practical experience.

7. **Language Immersion through Real-Life Activities**
Students participate in **campus-based activities** like writing journals, reading aloud, or performing skits in English, which helps them practice language skills in real-world contexts.

To ensure the success of these activity-based approaches, Prof. Samanta encourages teachers to engage in regular skill enhancement through workshops and collaborative discussions. He emphasizes creating a welcoming, inclusive environment where students actively participate in their learning journey.

Inspirational tagline of him
"Active Minds, Engaged Hands: Empowering Education Through Real-Life Activities."

Role of Teachers at KISS: Shaping Future Citizens
"Today's child is tomorrow's citizen." If a child remains confined within the four walls of their family, their perspective becomes limited. To address this, schools provide a broader environment where children develop desirable attitudes and outlooks for social life. As the **Education Commission (1966)** aptly observed:
"The destiny of India is being shaped in her classrooms."

This profound statement underscores the critical role of schools as formal and active agencies of education, bridging the gap between a child's early life and their integration into the larger community. Within this structure, the teacher is pivotal.

The Teacher: A Central Figure in Education
Teachers play the most significant role in nurturing students into responsible and capable citizens. They are not merely facilitators of knowledge but also architects of a child's character and outlook. The **Secondary Education Commission (1952-53)** highlighted this by stating:

"The most important factor in the contemplated educational reconstruction is the teacher—their personal qualities, educational qualifications, professional training, and the place they occupy in the school and community."

Similarly, the **Education Commission (1964-66)** emphasized:

"Of all the factors influencing the quality of education and contributing to material development, the competence and character of the teacher are undoubtedly the most important."

These words resonate deeply at KISS, where teachers are the real practitioners of the teaching-learning process and the bedrock of the institution's success.

Teachers at KISS: Multi-Dimensional Role

At KISS, teachers are more than educators; they are caregivers, mentors, and facilitators of holistic development. The institution thrives under their dedicated efforts to nurture tribal children, transforming them into confident and skilled individuals. Their multi-dimensional role includes:

- Acting as **guides** to impart moral and ethical values.
- Serving as **mentors**, shaping the personalities of students through active engagement.
- Functioning as **facilitators** in experiential and activity-based learning tailored to the students' unique contexts.
- Playing a **parental role**, ensuring the emotional and psychological well-being of every child.

Their efforts extend beyond classrooms, with active involvement in co-curricular, vocational, and social programs that equip students with life skills, making them not just educated individuals but valuable contributors to society.

Teachers as "Gardeners" at KISS

Prof. Achyuta Samanta often likens teachers at KISS to gardeners in a vast and vibrant garden, nurturing each child—like a delicate sapling—with care and dedication. Through their consistent hard work and innovative teaching methods, teachers ensure that KISS shines not just nationally but also internationally.

Inspirational tagline of him

"Inspiring Minds, Building Futures: The Teacher's Role at KISS."
Let us discuss the multi-dimensional roles of the teachers, which illustrated this institution:

1. Role as Teacher

In the context of **holistic education**, the role of the teacher at KISS is not confined to mere delivery of academic content but extends to fostering a nurturing environment where students' cognitive, emotional, and social development is equally prioritized. **Prof. Samanta Sir's educational philosophy** emphasizes that **responsible teaching** goes beyond teaching subjects—it is about guiding students to become well-rounded individuals capable of critical thinking, empathy, and active participation in their communities.

Classroom Teaching as a Motivational Process

At KISS, teachers understand that motivation is key to engaging students in the learning process. The teacher's role is to inspire curiosity and a love for learning by creating an atmosphere where students feel valued, respected, and encouraged to explore their interests. Teachers motivate students not only through words but through their actions—acting as role models, displaying a passion for learning, and creating an environment where students are encouraged to ask questions, think critically, and approach learning with enthusiasm.

Building Connections and Promoting Active Learning

The teaching process at KISS is designed to engage students actively, connecting lessons to real-life experiences, cultural contexts, and the students' own backgrounds. This is where the holistic approach comes into play—the teacher is responsible for making learning meaningful by relating academic concepts to the students' lived experiences, helping them understand how knowledge applies to their daily lives.

By establishing these connections, teachers foster an environment where students are not passive receivers of information but active participants in their learning journey. Teachers at KISS work to build critical thinking and problem-solving skills, encouraging students to engage with the material actively, reflect on their experiences, and develop a sense of responsibility for their own learning.

Guiding and Supporting Emotional Growth

Teachers at KISS understand that the emotional development of a student is as important as their intellectual development. Recognizing the diverse backgrounds and life experiences of tribal students, teachers are equipped with the empathy and patience to support students through their unique challenges. This emotional support helps students build self-confidence and a positive self-image, both essential components of a holistic education.

In this environment, teachers not only teach academic subjects but also serve as mentors and counselors, helping students navigate challenges, overcome insecurities, and develop emotional intelligence. By fostering a positive and supportive classroom environment, teachers at KISS ensure that students feel safe and empowered to express themselves, take risks in their learning, and build the resilience they need to succeed.

Creating a Responsible and Inclusive Learning Environment

Prof. Samanta Sir's holistic education philosophy stresses the importance of **inclusive education**—teaching that acknowledges and values the diverse needs, abilities, and backgrounds of all students. Teachers at KISS are not only educators but also **advocates** for the success of every student. They are responsible for creating a classroom culture where all students, regardless of their backgrounds or learning styles, are included and respected. Teachers provide individual attention, adapt their teaching methods to cater to various learning needs, and create a sense of community within the classroom.

Encouraging Lifelong Learning and Responsibility

A key aspect of responsible teaching is fostering a mindset of **lifelong learning**. Teachers at KISS motivate students to be curious and persistent learners—instilling in them the importance of learning beyond the classroom. By guiding students to explore, question, and critically analyze, teachers prepare them to face challenges both within and outside the classroom. Through their active role as facilitators, mentors, and motivators, teachers at KISS help students become responsible, self-reliant individuals capable of continuing their educational journey long after they leave school.

2. Role as a Mentor

In the framework of **holistic education**, the role of a teacher extends beyond classroom instruction to one of a **mentor** who nurtures the all-around development of students. At KISS, teachers not only provide academic guidance but also serve as emotional and social mentors, fostering an environment where students feel valued, understood, and supported. This mentoring relationship is integral to the institution's philosophy of developing students into well-rounded, responsible, and compassionate individuals.

Mentoring Beyond Academics

At KISS, teachers take a **personalized approach** to mentoring, understanding that the needs of students are not limited to their academic progress. Teachers frequently engage with students in both formal and informal settings, such as visiting their rooms, having one-on-one discussions, and sharing life experiences. These interactions are designed to build trust and create a safe space where students can express their concerns and challenges freely. Whether it is related to **studies, health, social issues, or personal difficulties**, teachers listen with empathy and provide appropriate guidance, offering students the emotional support they need to thrive.

Building Trust and Emotional Support

A key element of the teacher-student relationship at KISS is the creation of a **nurturing and supportive environment**. As mentors, teachers go beyond their role as educators—they act as **guides, counselors, and sometimes even parental figures** for their students. By closely interacting with students and being approachable, teachers at KISS make sure that the students feel comfortable enough to share their personal experiences and struggles. This deep emotional connection helps students feel safe, understood, and empowered to work through their challenges.

Academic and Career Guidance

Teachers at KISS also serve as career and academic advisors, offering **personalized mentorship** to help students set goals, identify their strengths, and plan for their future. They understand the aspirations of their students and help them chart a path towards achieving those goals. Whether it's advice on pursuing higher education, choosing a career,  or developing specific skills, teachers at KISS are always available to guide students in making informed decisions about their academic and professional futures.

Holistic Development through Mentorship

In line with **holistic education**, mentoring at KISS focuses on the **whole child**—intellectual, emotional, social, and moral development. Teachers at KISS actively help students develop life skills such as critical thinking, decision-making, and emotional intelligence. They promote not just academic success, but the development of **character, resilience**, and a sense of **social responsibility**. Mentors encourage students to participate in both **curricular** and **co-curricular activities**, thereby ensuring that their personal growth is as prioritized as their academic achievements.

Creating a Sense of Belonging and Responsibility

The teacher-mentor relationship at KISS fosters a strong sense of **belonging** among students. By creating opportunities for open dialogue and supporting students through challenges, mentors help cultivate a **positive self-image** in students, promoting their confidence and self-esteem. Furthermore, teachers encourage students to take **responsibility** for their own learning and well-being, empowering them to make thoughtful decisions, set personal goals, and achieve success both inside and outside the classroom.

3. Role as Tutor

At KISS, as a **residential school**, teachers take on the important role of **tutors**, extending their support beyond the classroom to ensure the **holistic development** of every student. This is particularly significant in a setting where students come from diverse tribal backgrounds and live on campus, receiving their education completely free of cost. In this environment, teachers are not only responsible for academic instruction but also serve as accessible, constant sources of guidance for students, addressing their needs beyond formal teaching hours.

Guiding Beyond the Classroom

As **tutors**, teachers at KISS dedicate themselves to helping students **navigate their academic challenges** throughout the day, well beyond the scheduled class times. They provide **personalized support**, patiently guiding students through concepts they may not have fully grasped during regular lessons. This approach ensures that **students of all backgrounds**—especially those who may have gaps in prior education—receive the attention they need to succeed.

A Home Away from Home

KISS functions as a **second home** for tribal students, and the teachers' roles reflect the **nurturing and caring environment** that this institution strives to provide. Recognizing that students live on campus and are away from their families, teachers step into the role of **guardians** and mentors, offering support not only with academic tasks but also with personal challenges. This mentorship goes beyond helping with textbooks—it extends to guiding students through life's practicalities and difficulties, ensuring that they feel **safe, supported, and valued**.

Personalized Attention to Each Student's Needs

Teachers at KISS are committed to giving **individualized attention** to every student, helping them with their specific academic struggles. Whether it's in the form of one-on-one tutoring sessions, group study sessions, or additional guidance on projects, teachers make themselves available to ensure that no student falls behind. This attention is essential for **holistic development**, as it not only addresses academic needs but also builds **confidence**, **independence**, and **problem-solving skills**.

Fostering Academic Growth and Emotional Well-being

In the spirit of **holistic education**, the role of the tutor goes beyond intellectual development. Teachers at KISS work to create a **well-rounded learning environment**, where the academic and emotional well-being of students are equally prioritized. By fostering **a supportive atmosphere**, teachers help students manage stress, stay motivated, and cultivate a love for learning. They actively listen to students' concerns, offering academic help as well as emotional support when needed.

Promoting Self-Directed Learning

As part of their tutoring role, teachers at KISS encourage students to take **ownership of their learning**. They guide students in developing **self-directed learning** skills, helping them to become independent thinkers and learners. Teachers provide the tools and resources students need to solve problems on their own, instilling in them a **sense of responsibility** for their own educational journey.

Encouraging Collaborative Learning

Teachers also foster an environment of **collaborative learning**, encouraging students to work together and support one another. Through study groups and peer tutoring, students learn the value of **teamwork** and **community**, which are key principles in holistic education. This approach helps students develop **social skills**, **empathy**, and a sense of **collective responsibility**.

Inspirational tagline of him

"Tutoring with Care, Teaching with Heart: Empowering Students for a Brighter Future at KISS."

4. Role in Dining based duty and Roaster

Kalinga Institute of Social Sciences (KISS), a world-class residential institution, serves as a home to over 30,000 tribal students within a single campus. Managing the dining operations in such a vast institution is far more complex than running a small kitchen in a traditional school setting. It demands meticulous planning, coordination, and dedicated involvement from all stakeholders, especially the teachers.

At KISS, teachers play an indispensable role in ensuring the smooth functioning of dining services on a daily basis. Their responsibilities extend beyond mere supervision and encompass the following key areas:

Guiding Student Behavior:

Teachers take charge of organizing students during mealtime by instructing them on seating arrangements and maintaining discipline in the dining area. This ensures an orderly environment where every student can have their meal without confusion or delay.

Monitoring Food Distribution:

Teachers oversee the serving process, ensuring that food servers provide meals adequately and equally to all students. They ensure no child is overlooked and that every student receives sufficient and nutritious food.

Daily Dining List Preparation:

A vital part of the teacher's responsibility is preparing the daily dining list, which includes monitoring student attendance and accommodating any special dietary requirements. This helps streamline the distribution process and minimizes food wastage.

Quality Assurance:

Teachers consistently inspect the quality of food served, ensuring it meets the nutritional and safety standards required for growing children. Their vigilant oversight guarantees that students receive wholesome, hygienic meals every day.

Ensuring No Child Goes Hungry:

One of the most significant roles of teachers is to ensure that no student goes hungry. They actively address any gaps in the system and take corrective measures promptly to meet the needs of all students.

The role of teachers in running the dining system at KISS reflects the institution's commitment to holistic care and community well-being. The dining hall is more than a place for meals; it is a space where the values of discipline, equality, and mutual respect are nurtured. Teachers embody these values through their active participation, demonstrating a philosophy rooted in the educational ethos of Dr. Achyuta Samanta, the visionary founder of KISS.

Dr. Samanta's philosophy emphasizes the holistic development of students, where education extends beyond academics to include physical well-being, emotional nurturing, and moral grounding. The involvement of teachers in dining duties exemplifies this philosophy in action, as they contribute not just as educators but as caregivers and role models for the students.

In conclusion, the seamless operation of dining services at KISS is a testament to the dedication and coordinated efforts of teachers. Their unwavering commitment ensures that each child, irrespective of their background, receives care, nourishment, and dignity—an embodiment of the inclusive and transformative vision of KISS.

5. Role as supervisor

In the holistic educational model envisioned by Dr. Achyuta Samanta, teachers are not merely instructors but also dynamic supervisors who ensure the seamless functioning of various facets of institutional life. This supervision extends beyond the boundaries of classrooms, reflecting a philosophy that prioritizes the all-around development of students.

Teachers at KISS serve as supervisors in diverse areas, playing a pivotal role in:

1. Curricular and Co-Curricular Activities:

Teachers actively oversee the academic progress and participation of students, ensuring that learning is engaging, inclusive, and tailored to meet the individual needs of each learner. They also encourage students to partake in co-curricular pursuits such as arts, cultural events, and creative competitions, fostering well-rounded personalities.

2. Hostel Management and Discipline:

The hostel serves as a second home for students, and teachers take on the role of guardians by supervising cleanliness, hygiene, and orderliness in the living spaces. They ensure that students develop habits of personal and environmental cleanliness, which are vital life skills.

3.   **Study Hours and Vocational Activities:**
Teachers ensure that hostel study hours are utilized effectively, promoting a disciplined and focused learning environment. Additionally, they oversee vocational activities, which impart practical skills and foster self-reliance among students, aligning with Dr. Samanta's vision of empowering marginalized communities.

4.   **Sports and Games Supervision:**
Recognizing the importance of physical education, teachers supervise sports and games, ensuring active participation and fair play. This not only contributes to physical fitness but also instills values like teamwork, perseverance, and leadership in students.

5.   **Observations and Celebrations:**
Teachers play a critical supervisory role in organizing institutional observances, festivals, and events. They guide students in understanding the significance of these occasions, fostering a sense of community, cultural appreciation, and shared responsibility.

Through their multifaceted supervisory roles, teachers embody the core tenets of Dr. Samanta's educational philosophy: care, discipline, and holistic development. Their contributions reflect the institution's commitment to nurturing confident, compassionate, and capable individuals who are well-prepared for life's challenges.

In this model, the teacher is not just an academic guide but a mentor, role model, and pillar of support, embodying the transformative vision of education that KISS stands for.

6.   Role as Organiser

At KISS, the role of teachers as organizers is integral to the institution's mission of providing holistic education and transformative experiences for students. Guided by the visionary philosophy of Dr. Achyuta Samanta, the teachers' responsibilities in organizing various functions and events go beyond logistical arrangements—they serve as enablers of meaningful exposure, skill-building, and character development.

Facilitating Global Exposure:

KISS regularly hosts a wide range of functions and events, stemming from its global reputation and the interest of dignitaries and visitors from across the world. These occasions provide students with unparalleled opportunities to interact with global leaders, understand diverse perspectives, and showcase their cultural heritage and talents. Teachers play a critical role in planning, coordinating, and executing these events seamlessly, ensuring they reflect the institution's ethos of excellence and inclusivity.

Encouraging Student Participation:

Teachers at KISS are committed to nurturing the talents and confidence of students by encouraging them to participate actively in curricular and co-curricular activities. Whether it is cultural programs, sports events, or academic competitions, teachers ensure that students gain enriching experiences that contribute to their personal growth and self-esteem.

Empowering Student-Led Initiatives:

In alignment with Dr. Samanta's philosophy of empowerment, teachers guide students to take ownership of organizing various programs such as seminars, NSS activities, cleanliness drives, and community service initiatives. By doing so, they instill leadership qualities, teamwork, and a sense of social responsibility in students, equipping them to become proactive contributors to society.

Organizing with Innovation and Dedication:

Teachers often take the initiative to organize programs through their creativity and dedication, bringing vibrancy and diversity to campus life. From cultural celebrations to vocational training workshops, their efforts reflect their commitment to holistic development.

Executing Institutional Plans:

One of the most critical responsibilities of teachers is implementing plans and policies formulated by the institution's leadership at the grassroots level. They ensure that every initiative, whether academic, cultural, or social, is executed effectively, aligning with the broader goals of providing a world-class education and fostering inclusivity and equity.

In the holistic educational philosophy of Dr. Achyuta Samanta, the teacher as an organizer represents a cornerstone of transformative education. Their role extends beyond facilitating events to creating experiences that enrich students' lives, build character, and prepare them to thrive in a global society.

By blending responsibility, innovation, and mentorship, teachers exemplify the values of care, inclusivity, and empowerment that define KISS, ensuring that every student benefits from a nurturing and dynamic environment.

7. Role as Controller

Effective planning and smooth control are the backbone of any successful organization, and this is particularly true for an institution as vast and diverse as Kalinga Institute of Social Sciences (KISS). In Dr. Achyuta Samanta's holistic educational philosophy, teachers play a pivotal role as controllers, ensuring that the institution runs seamlessly while nurturing the discipline and character of its students.

Control through Discipline and Care:

At KISS, the need for discipline among 25,000 tribal students living on one campus is paramount. Despite their vulnerable backgrounds, students are transformed into disciplined and responsible individuals under the guidance of their teachers. Teachers, through their close connection to students, serve as the ideal figures to instill a sense of discipline—not through authority but by earning trust and respect.

Proximity to Students' Hearts:

Teachers at KISS act as mentors, confidants, and role models for students. Their ability to connect with students at a personal level allows them to shape attitudes and behaviors effectively. By sharing life experiences, offering guidance, and demonstrating ethical behavior, teachers inspire students to follow rules and embrace discipline as a value integral to personal and communal growth.

Building a Culture of Self-Regulation:

Rather than imposing discipline externally, teachers at KISS help students develop self-discipline by fostering a culture of accountability, mutual respect, and empathy. Through consistent engagement in classrooms, hostels, and extracurricular activities, teachers empower students to take ownership of their actions and decisions.

Implementing Institutional Plans:

Teachers also play a critical role in executing institutional policies and plans. They ensure that the directives from higher authorities are implemented effectively at the grassroots level, creating a well-regulated environment. Their efforts maintain harmony and order in all aspects of campus life, from academics and sports to hostel management and event coordination.

Fostering Holistic Growth:

The control exerted by teachers is not limited to discipline but extends to the holistic development of students. By maintaining structure and order, teachers create an environment where students can thrive academically, socially, and emotionally. This aligns with Dr. Samanta's philosophy, which emphasizes education as a means to uplift marginalized communities and prepare them for global opportunities.

A Unique System of Control:

The smooth functioning of KISS, despite its size and diversity, is a testament to the unique control system spearheaded by teachers. They transform potential challenges into opportunities for growth and learning, proving that discipline and care go hand in hand in building a transformative educational ecosystem.

In conclusion, the teacher's role as a controller is central to the philosophy of Dr. Achyuta Samanta. By blending discipline with compassion, teachers ensure that KISS not only operates efficiently but also fulfills its mission of creating a disciplined, self-reliant, and empowered generation of learners. Their efforts are a living embodiment of the institution's values of care, inclusivity, and transformation.

8. Role as Planner

At KISS, teachers play a vital role as planners, contributing directly to the institution's mission of providing quality, need-based education. In Dr. Achyuta Samanta's holistic educational philosophy, teachers are not just implementers of policies but also active contributors to the planning process, ensuring that it aligns with the needs, aspirations, and potential of the students.

Providing Feedback for Effective Planning:

Teachers, as direct stakeholders and grassroots-level participants, bring invaluable insights to the planning process. Through their observations, experiences, and challenges faced in day-to-day interactions with students, teachers provide constructive feedback to institutional authorities and curriculum designers. This feedback is instrumental in formulating practical, engaging, and need-based plans that cater to the diverse needs of students.

Planning Curricular and Co-Curricular Activities:

In addition to supporting institutional planning, teachers independently plan and organize a wide range of curricular and co-curricular activities within the campus. These include monthly seminars, workshops, examination schedules, and other academic initiatives. Their meticulous planning ensures that these activities are purposeful, inclusive, and aligned with the holistic development goals of the institution.

Fostering Student-Centric Planning:

Teachers prioritize student interests and needs while formulating plans, ensuring that activities are both engaging and relevant. By understanding the unique challenges and aspirations of tribal students, they help design programs that foster academic excellence, cultural preservation, and social responsibility.

Balancing Structure and Flexibility:

As planners, teachers strike a balance between structure and flexibility. They ensure that while institutional goals are met, there is room for innovation and adaptability based on real-time feedback and situational requirements. This dynamic approach reflects the essence of Dr. Samanta's philosophy, which values practicality and responsiveness.

Empowering Through Participation:

Teachers also involve students in the planning process, encouraging them to contribute ideas and take ownership of activities. This participatory approach not only enhances the relevance of plans but also instills leadership and decision-making skills in students, preparing them for future responsibilities.

Integral to the Holistic Vision:

The role of teachers as planners is pivotal to the success of KISS's holistic educational model. By ensuring that all plans—whether academic, co-curricular, or administrative—are practical, student-focused, and need-based, teachers help create a nurturing and dynamic learning environment.

In Dr. Achyuta Samanta's philosophy, the teacher as a planner is more than a facilitator; they are visionaries who bridge the gap between institutional aspirations and grassroots realities. Their role exemplifies the transformative power of education in shaping lives and communities.

9. Role as Manager

Managing the world's largest residential educational institution like KISS requires a collaborative and systematic approach. Recognizing this, Dr. Achyuta Samanta has entrusted teachers with vital managerial responsibilities to ensure the effective and smooth functioning of the institution. In his holistic educational philosophy, teachers are seen as pivotal managers who bridge the gap between institutional authorities and students, fostering an environment of care, discipline, and growth.

Teachers as Managers:

Teachers at KISS take on diverse managerial roles to support the day-to-day operations of the institution. They act as intermediaries between the administration and students, ensuring that plans and policies are implemented effectively at the grassroots level. Their ability to connect with students on a personal level allows them to manage various aspects of campus life, including academics, hostels, co-curricular activities, and community initiatives.

Friend, Guide, and Philosopher:

Teachers at KISS are more than just managers; they serve as friends, guides, and philosophers to the students. By mentoring and supporting students, they help them navigate academic and personal challenges, foster a sense of responsibility, and instill values that prepare them for life beyond the campus.

Collaborative Leadership:

In Dr. Samanta's vision, the success of KISS is rooted in teamwork and shared responsibility. Teachers play a critical role in this model, working alongside administrators and other stakeholders to manage resources, resolve issues, and create a nurturing environment. Their leadership ensures that the institution runs efficiently despite its vast size and complexity.

Acknowledgment of Teachers' Contributions:

Dr. Samanta has always emphasized the invaluable contributions of teachers to the success of KISS. He acknowledges that the institution's remarkable achievements would not have been possible without their dedication and unwavering commitment. By entrusting them with managerial roles, he not only ensures effective management but also honors their indispensable role in shaping the lives of thousands of students.

A Pillar of Holistic Education:

The role of teachers as managers is integral to the holistic educational philosophy of KISS. Their ability to balance administrative duties with their responsibilities as mentors and educators ensures that the institution remains a beacon of excellence. Their efforts exemplify the transformative power of education and highlight the importance of collaboration in achieving institutional success.

In conclusion, the teachers' role as managers underscores the ethos of shared leadership and dedication at KISS. Their contributions, celebrated by Dr. Samanta, are a testament to the profound impact of compassionate and effective management in building a world-class institution.

Holistic education and Student

In Dr. Achyuta Samanta's holistic educational philosophy, the child is considered the "main character" or "hero" in the transformative journey of education. He emphasizes that education exists for the child, not the other way around. This student-centered philosophy prioritizes the natural development, freedom, and well-being of the child over rigid educational structures or societal expectations.

Child-Centered Approach:

Dr. Samanta believes that every child should be treated as a child, not as a miniature adult, within the educational environment. Acknowledging the innocence and purity of the child at birth, he views children as untarnished souls, inherently free from societal evils. However, external influences—such as poverty, caste, religion, and cultural pressures—often corrupt and hinder the child's natural growth. To counter this, he envisions an education system that shields children from such societal ills, fostering their development in a modern, progressive, and nurturing environment.

Education for Holistic Development:

Dr. Samanta asserts that education should aim to develop the child as a whole, encompassing intellectual, emotional, physical, and moral growth. He believes that the learning environment should align with the child's innate nature and capabilities, enabling them to flourish naturally without undue pressure or constraints.

Empowering Tribal Children:

Recognizing the unique challenges faced by tribal children, who are often marginalized and shy by nature, Dr. Samanta provides them with a supportive and natural setting. He ensures that these children feel safe, respected, and free to express themselves, which helps to unlock their hidden potential. His philosophy emphasizes equal opportunities and inclusivity, enabling tribal children to thrive despite their socio-economic and cultural challenges.

Inspired by Philosophical Foundations:

Dr. Samanta's approach resonates with the educational philosophies of great thinkers:

- **Jean-Jacques Rousseau's** belief in the natural goodness of children and the importance of providing them a free and natural environment for learning.
- **John Dewey's** emphasis on education as a tool for personal and social growth, grounded in real-life experiences.
- **Mahatma Gandhi's** vision of education as a means to empower the individual while nurturing moral and ethical values.

A Progressive Vision:

Dr. Samanta's philosophy aligns with the belief that education should be a liberating force, enabling children to rise above societal constraints and develop their full potential. By fostering an environment free from prejudice, discrimination, and undue rigidity, he seeks to create empowered individuals who can lead meaningful lives and contribute to a better society.

In conclusion, Dr. Achyuta Samanta's child-centered educational philosophy places the student at the heart of the educational process. By nurturing their innate abilities and shielding them from societal ills, he redefines education as a tool for holistic and transformative development, particularly for marginalized communities. This approach ensures that every child, regardless of background, has the opportunity to thrive and become a positive force in society.

Holistic education and School

In Dr. Achyuta Samanta's holistic educational philosophy, the school is regarded as a "miniature society," a sacred space where education transcends the mere transfer of knowledge. It is a dynamic environment for cultivating moral values, social skills, and universal brotherhood, preparing students to contribute meaningfully to society while realizing their full potential.

School as a Nurturing Ground:

Dr. Samanta emphasizes that a school is not just a place for imparting knowledge for its own sake; it is a transformative space where children are prepared to face life with resilience, empathy, and a sense of responsibility. It serves as a foundation for nurturing the hidden talents and innate potential within each child, offering them the tools and opportunities needed for holistic growth.

Cultivating Moral Values and Brotherhood:

According to Dr. Samanta, the school is a sacred place where moral values are sown and universal brotherhood is cultivated. By fostering respect for diversity and encouraging compassion, the school environment helps students develop a sense of unity and interconnectedness, transcending barriers of caste, religion, and socio-economic status.

Preparing Future Leaders:

The school is envisioned as a place for shaping the leaders of tomorrow. It not only equips students with academic knowledge but also instills a strong sense of national and cultural identity. Dr. Samanta believes that education should integrate a country's own ideology and heritage, enabling students to lead with confidence, integrity, and a commitment to societal progress.

Inspired by Holistic Philosophies:

Dr. Samanta's vision aligns with several key educational philosophies:
- **John Dewey's** view of the school as a microcosm of society, where students learn to interact, collaborate, and develop socially responsible behavior.
- **Rabindranath Tagore's** emphasis on nurturing creativity and individuality in an environment of freedom and harmony.
- **Swami Vivekananda's** ideal of education as the manifestation of the perfection already present in every individual, combined with the cultivation of moral and spiritual values.

A Place for Inclusive Growth:

For Dr. Samanta, a school must be inclusive, ensuring that children from all backgrounds, especially marginalized and tribal communities, feel valued and supported. By creating an environment of mutual respect and encouragement, schools can become agents of empowerment and social transformation.

School as a Catalyst for Holistic Education:

In line with his philosophy, the school becomes a platform where students evolve not just academically but also emotionally, socially, and ethically. It is where their intellect is sharpened, their creativity unleashed, and their character shaped.

In conclusion, Dr. Achyuta Samanta's holistic view of the school places it at the heart of societal and individual transformation. It is not merely a center for learning but a sacred space for cultivating virtues, nurturing potential, and preparing future generations to lead with compassion and purpose. This philosophy underscores the vital role of schools in building a progressive, inclusive, and harmonious society.

Discipline

In Dr. Achyuta Samanta's educational philosophy, discipline is redefined as an intrinsic quality that emerges naturally through freedom, rather than something imposed externally. He advocates for granting children full freedom to explore, learn, and express themselves creatively. This freedom, he believes, is essential for the child's holistic development, self-discovery, and the realization of their innate potential.

Freedom as a Catalyst for Growth:

Dr. Samanta asserts that freedom is a necessary condition for natural growth and self-realization. When children are free to pursue their interests and manifest their creativity, they develop organically as independent and well-rounded individuals. This perspective resonates with the philosophies of:

- **Jean-Jacques Rousseau,** who emphasized the importance of freedom and natural development in a child's education.
- **Rabindranath Tagore,** who believed that children flourish in an environment of creativity and freedom rather than rigid discipline.

Self-Discipline Over External Discipline:

While Dr. Samanta does not support external discipline, which he views as an impediment to a child's natural development, he strongly advocates for self-discipline. He believes that when children are nurtured in a free and

creative environment, they internalize discipline as a personal responsibility. This aligns with the educational ideas of:
- **Maria Montessori,** who emphasized self-discipline developed through structured freedom and independent activities.
- **Mahatma Gandhi,** who stressed self-restraint and personal responsibility as essential elements of discipline.

Tutor-Mentoring Approach:

To cultivate self-discipline, Dr. Samanta has introduced innovative methods such as tutor-mentoring at KISS. Through close guidance, mentorship, and real participation in diverse activities, children learn to manage their own behaviors and actions effectively. This personalized approach fosters mutual respect and accountability, creating a foundation for lifelong discipline.

Role of Teachers in Fostering Discipline:

Dr. Samanta advises teachers to adopt a compassionate, patient, and respectful attitude toward children. He cautions against being arbitrary, despotic, or ill-tempered, as such behaviors can undermine the child's sense of self-worth and hinder their natural growth. Instead, teachers are encouraged to recognize the divinity within every child and assist them in becoming conscious of their potential. This aligns with the philosophies of:
- **Swami Vivekananda,** who believed in respecting the inherent divinity and potential within every individual.
- **John Dewey,** who advocated for participatory and experiential learning as a means of fostering self-regulation.

Freedom as a Path to True Discipline:

Dr. Samanta emphasizes that when children are taught in an atmosphere of complete freedom, they naturally develop discipline. A free, creative, and inclusive environment allows children to explore their interests, understand the value of rules, and cultivate self-regulation without external enforcement.

Conclusion:

In Dr. Achyuta Samanta's holistic philosophy, discipline is not about control but about enabling children to grow freely and responsibly. By fostering an environment of freedom, respect, and creativity, he ensures that children develop self-discipline organically, paving the way for their holistic development and the realization of their potential as compassionate and self-aware individuals. This approach underscores the transformative power of education in shaping not just disciplined individuals but responsible, empathetic members of society.

Contribution of Prof. Achyuta Samanta to the Current Indian Education System

Prof. Achyuta Samanta has made groundbreaking contributions to the modern Indian education system, bringing a significant transformation in various aspects of education. His educational philosophy, innovative methods, and progressive vision have brought about considerable changes in the aims, methods, curriculum, teacher roles, and nature of discipline, all of which are aligned with the needs of contemporary India. His work is highly relevant to reconstructing Indian culture and heritage, fostering the holistic development of students, and addressing the needs of marginalized communities. Below are the major contributions of Prof. Samanta Sir:

1. **Holistic Development of Students**:

Prof. Samanta emphasizes the all-round development of students, focusing on physical, intellectual, moral, social, and spiritual growth. This approach aligns with the Indian ethos of nurturing the complete individual, ensuring that students develop their innate abilities in all these areas. His emphasis on holistic development has a profound relevance for shaping well-rounded, responsible citizens in today's society.

2. **Adoption of Child-Centered Educational Methods**:

Prof. Samanta has been a staunch advocate of integrating modern advances in educational psychology, particularly child-centered approaches to teaching. These methods prioritize the psychological development of the child and encourage active, experiential learning, helping students to engage meaningfully with the content and become active participants in their education.

3. **Promotion of Honesty, Morality, and Good Conduct**:

In a time when corruption and dishonesty often plague Indian society, Prof. Samanta has consistently emphasized the values of honesty, morality, impartiality, and integrity. He believes these are the summum bonum (highest ideals) of life, and he holds teachers to the highest standards of ethical conduct, ensuring that the values of truthfulness and morality are upheld in educational settings.

4. **Re-establishment of Teacher-Student Relationships**:

Prof. Samanta has revived the ancient Gurukul system of education, fostering a close, mentor-like relationship between teachers and students.

This relationship is fundamental to the smooth functioning of KISS, where over 25,000 students live and learn together without incidents of indiscipline. His model serves as a testament to the power of compassionate and dedicated teaching in managing large institutions.

5. **Universal Education for Vulnerable Groups**:

    Prof. Samanta is a pioneer in providing quality education to vulnerable and underdeveloped tribal children. His vision aligns with the universalization of education and the government's efforts to reach marginalized communities, particularly Scheduled Tribes (STs) and Scheduled Castes (SCs). His work with tribal children has been transformative, ensuring that these communities receive the education they deserve to break the cycles of poverty.

6. **Curriculum Development Focused on National and Societal Needs**:

    Prof. Samanta's educational philosophy emphasizes creating curricula that are relevant to the needs of India and society. His curriculum is practical and need-based, considering both the interests of students and the demands of the community. This ensures that students are not only academically equipped but also socially responsible and prepared for real-world challenges.

7. **Vocational Education and Skill Development**:

    Prof. Samanta's curriculum is deeply rooted in vocational training, enabling students to become self-sufficient after completing their education. By integrating vocational education into the general curriculum, Prof. Samanta has made it a successful model, something that had been attempted but failed previously. His efforts are in line with the vision of Mahatma Gandhi, who advocated for integrating vocational education with general education, and have proven successful in providing meaningful employment to students.

8. **Promotion of Democratic Ideals and Citizenship Development**:

    Prof. Samanta encourages students to actively participate in democratic processes and engage in various co-curricular activities like NSS, NCC, Scouts, and Guides. These activities help students develop a sense of responsibility, leadership, and citizenship, which is essential for the growth of democratic values in society.

9. **Fostering International Standards in Sports and Physical Education**:

    Prof. Samanta recognizes the importance of physical education and sports in a child's development. By emphasizing physical fitness alongside academics, he has created a system where students excel in international sports competitions, including the Olympics. His belief in "a sound mind in a sound body" is exemplified at KISS, where students regularly participate in athletic events and have achieved remarkable success.

10. **Collaboration with Industry for Skill Development:**
Prof. Samanta has worked tirelessly to ensure that students acquire the skills necessary to thrive in the modern job market. He has established collaborations with organizations like IL&FS, TCS, PMKVY, and others, providing students with industrial training that bridges the gap between education and employment.

11. **Integration of Life Skills and Health Education:**
In addition to academic and vocational training, Prof. Samanta places significant importance on life skills education. He ensures that students are equipped with essential skills like communication, problem-solving, and interpersonal skills, which are crucial for personal and professional success. His health education programs, addressing global issues like HIV/AIDS and malaria, have made a profound impact on the well-being of tribal communities.

12. **Women's Education and Empowerment:**
Prof. Samanta has been a staunch advocate for women's education, particularly in marginalized tribal communities. By admitting 60% of tribal girls to KISS, he has empowered them to lead their families and communities towards a brighter future. His commitment to gender equality is demonstrated through his efforts to provide quality education to girls, where literacy rates are still low.

13. **Innovative Social Programs:**
Prof. Samanta has launched several initiatives to uplift the underprivileged. Programs like "New Mind, New Dream" (NUA MANA NUA SAPANA), "KAMPASHN" (a charitable store for used goods), and "The Art of Giving" (a philosophy aimed at global peace) are examples of his efforts to create a harmonious society.

14. **Health Education and Sustainable Development:**
Prof. Samanta has responded to the Millennium Development Goals (MDGs) by focusing on issues such as poverty, gender equality, and environmental sustainability. His efforts in tribal health education have made a significant impact on reducing child mortality rates and combating diseases prevalent in tribal areas.

15. **International Recognition and Best Practices:**
Prof. Samanta's work has been recognized globally, with KISS receiving praise from governments and international organizations, including the United Nations. His model of education has been hailed as one of the best residential educational systems, providing a holistic environment for learning and growth.

Prof. Achyuta Samanta's contributions to the Indian education system are immense and multifaceted. His work is grounded in the belief that education should be holistic, inclusive, and aligned with the needs of society. By creating a comprehensive educational model that addresses the intellectual, physical, moral, and social development of students, he has set a new standard for education in India, particularly for tribal and marginalized communities. Prof. Samanta's vision has not only transformed the lives of thousands of students but has also had a lasting impact on the future of Indian education.

Conclusion

In conclusion, the Kalinga Institute of Social Sciences (KISS) stands as a living testament to the transformative power of education, particularly for marginalized tribal communities. Under the visionary leadership of Prof. Achyuta Samanta, KISS has grown from a single institution into a global educational network, with branches not only across the state of Odisha but also in other parts of India, such as Delhi and Chhattisgarh, and international collaborations with countries like Britain, Sri Lanka, Bangladesh, and Bhutan. Prof. Samanta's relentless dedication to empowering tribal children with progressive, need-based, and holistic education has led to the establishment of 29 nodal centers in Odisha alone, with plans for further expansion into tribal-dominated regions like Jharkhand and the North-Eastern states of India.

This holistic approach to education—focusing not only on intellectual development but also on physical, moral, social, and spiritual growth—aligns with the larger vision of creating well-rounded individuals who can contribute to the socio-economic development of their communities and the nation. Prof. Samanta's work is grounded in the belief that education should be inclusive, practical, and aligned with the needs of the learners and the society at large. His efforts have ensured that tribal children receive an education that is not just academic but also vocational, empowering them with skills for self-reliance and sustainable livelihoods.

Moreover, KISS's recognition by the United Nations with a special consultative status further underscores the global significance of Prof. Samanta's work. This distinction acknowledges the impactful contributions KISS has made in mainstreaming tribal education and fostering cross-cultural collaboration in the pursuit of educational equality. Prof. Samanta's dream of providing every tribal child with the opportunity for quality education, while honoring their cultural identity and values, has truly begun to take shape on a global scale.

As KISS continues to grow and evolve, its mission remains clear: to provide tribal communities with the tools, knowledge, and values they need to thrive in an increasingly complex and interconnected world. The legacy of KISS, and of Prof. Samanta's visionary leadership, is a beacon of hope for marginalized communities, inspiring future generations of educators and leaders who will continue this noble endeavor.

With this holistic educational philosophy, we hope that KISS, under Prof. Samanta's guidance, will evolve into a global center of excellence for tribal education, where every child, regardless of their background, can achieve their full potential and contribute to the betterment of society at large. Through the continuous pursuit of this vision, KISS will remain a transformative force, shaping the future of tribal education both in India and beyond.

Comprehensive and Differential Comparison between Holistic and Integral Education

Aspect	Holistic Education	Integral Education
Core Philosophy	Develops the whole person by integrating intellectual, emotional, social, and physical growth.	Focuses on the total transformation of the individual, emphasizing the development of the Psychic Being (the true inner self) for spiritual growth.
Focus	Emphasis on balance across different dimensions of a person's life: academic, emotional, social, and physical.	Aims at spiritual evolution through the Psychic Being, transforming the individual to align with higher consciousness.
Role of Teacher	Acts as a guide and facilitator, helping students connect academic learning with practical life skills.	Acts as a spiritual guide, facilitating the awakening of the Psychic Being, leading students towards inner growth and self-realization.
Integration of Spirituality	Focuses on values, ethical development, and emotional intelligence with a more secular approach.	Spirituality is central; the teacher helps students develop their Psychic Being and connect to universal divine truths.
Goal of Education	To develop well-rounded individuals who can navigate life's challenges effectively with a balance of intellect and emotional intelligence.	To achieve self-realization through the development of the Psychic Being, aligning the individual's consciousness with divine knowledge and higher purpose.
Psychic Being	Not explicitly emphasized. Focus is on intellectual and emotional development.	Central to the educational process, the Psychic Being is the divine essence within each person, guiding the transformation of mind, emotions, and spirit.

Aspect	Holistic Education	Integral Education
Practical Applications	Applied in progressive schools with an emphasis on experiential learning, community involvement, and life skills integration.	Used in institutions influenced by Sri Aurobindo's philosophy, such as Auroville, where yoga, meditation, and spiritual practices support the development of the Psychic Being.
Methods of Learning	Includes project-based learning, collaborative activities, and emotional learning.	Focuses on meditation, yoga, and spiritual practices designed to awaken the Psychic Being, leading to inner transformation.

This table clarifies that Integral Education places significant emphasis on the development of the Psychic Being, with spiritual practices such as meditation and yoga playing a central role in guiding the individual toward inner transformation and alignment with a higher consciousness. The focus is on spiritual evolution and self-realization through the awakening of the Psychic Being, which is considered the true inner essence of the individual. The educational process is aimed at integrating the physical, mental, emotional, and spiritual aspects, aligning them with divine truth and universal consciousness.

On the other hand, Holistic Education seeks to develop the whole person but with a broader focus that does not center specifically on spirituality or the Psychic Being. It integrates intellectual, emotional, social, and physical growth, aiming to nurture well-rounded individuals. The emphasis is on balance, developing emotional intelligence, life skills, and ethical values, and preparing students to engage meaningfully in society. At KISS (Kalinga Institute of Social Sciences), Achyuta Samanta has redefined holistic education through his 3H's (Heart, Head, and Hand), 3R's (Reading, Writing, and Arithmetic), and 3E's (Educate, Empower, Enable) model, making it a comprehensive framework. This model prepares the best individuals by focusing on all aspects of personal growth and providing an education that is not only academic but also socially, emotionally, and ethically grounded, ensuring the creation of well-rounded, capable individuals ready for the challenges of the world.

BIBLIOGRAPHY

- Forbes, S. H. (2003). Holistic education: An analysis of its ideas and nature. Brandon Publishing, p- 5-10
- John Dewey (1921), Reconstruction in philosophy, University of London press ltd, p-38.
- Krishnamurti, J. (1953). Education and the significance of life. HarperCollins, p-35-40.
- Miller, R. (2000). Caring for New Life: Essays on Holistic Education. Foundation for Educational Renewal, p- 15-22.
- Noddings, N. (2013). Education and democracy in the 21st century. Teachers College Press, p-50-55.
- Rusk, R.R. (1956), Philosophical Bases of Education, London University of London Press p-56.
- Samuel Ravi, S. (2011), A comprehensive Study of education, PHI Learning Private Ltd., New Delhi p-167-172.
- Taneja, V. R. (2012), Educational Thought and Practice, Sterling Publishers Pvt. Ltd., New Delhi, p-137-145.
- Saxena, N.R. (2014), Philosophical and sociological Foundations of Education, r. Lall Book Depot, Meerut, UP, p-113.
- UNESCO. (2015). Rethinking education: Towards a global common good? Paris: UNESCO Publishing, p-28-32.

Web Sources:

http://www.achyutasamanta.com/
http://www.achyutasamanta.com/biodata.html
http://www.achyutasamanta.com/profile_full.html
http://www.achyutasamanta.com/biodata_full.html
https://books.google.co.in/books?id=X3SmelDOkBUC&pg=PR27&lpg=PR27&dq=philosophy+of+education+from+book+ravi+s+samuel&source=bl&ots=oFQo7-XO-x&sig=QNAdMafsgTcYFnsoLK5vtiBGEp-A&hl=en&sa=X&ved=0CDIQ6AEwBGoVChMI-oSL3aDuxwIVQxqOCh3PyQj5#v=onepage&q=philosophy%20of%20education%20from%20book%20ravi%20s%20samuel&f=false
https://books.google.co.in/books?id=X3SmelDOkBUC&pg=PA218&source=gbs_toc_r&cad=3#v=onepage&q&f=false
http://www.holistic-education.net/visitors.htm
https://en.wikipedia.org/wiki/Holistic_education

Black Eagle Books

www.blackeaglebooks.org
info@blackeaglebooks.org

Black Eagle Books, an independent publisher, was founded as a nonprofit organization in April, 2019. It is our mission to connect and engage the Indian diaspora and the world at large with the best of works of world literature published on a collaborative platform, with special emphasis on foregrounding Contemporary Classics and New Writing.

www.ingramcontent.com/pod-product-compliance
Lightning Source LLC
Chambersburg PA
CBHW080323080526
44585CB00021B/2449